Discovering AWARENESS

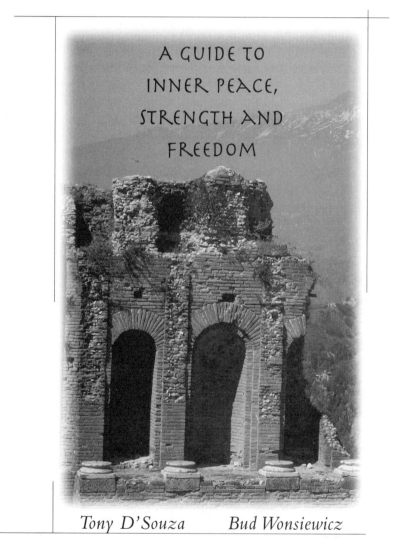

A GUIDE TO
INNER PEACE,
STRENGTH AND
FREEDOM

Tony D'Souza   *Bud Wonsiewicz*

BROADBAND LIVING PRESS

Designed by Ann W. Douden

Cover photograph by Michelle Maloy Dillon, MMD Photography

Packaged by Betsy R. Armstrong

Manufactured in Canada by Friesens

Library of Congress Control Number: 2006935677

ISBN 978-0-9790304-0-6

BROADBAND LIVING PRESS

A division of Broadband Living Unlimited LLC

www.BroadbandLiving.org

A set of audio guided meditations,
   Discovering Awareness: Guided Meditations,
   is available at www.BroadbandLiving.org

For more information about Broadband Living Press,
   contact info@BroadbandLiving.org

1 2 3 4 5 6 7 8 9 0

All net income from this book will be donated to charity.

DEDICATION

We dedicate this book to those who helped form us,

particularly Fr. Anthony De Mello, S. J.,

mentor, guide and friend.

ACKNOWLEDGMENTS

The authors wish to thank Fr. Robert de Rouen, S.J., who introduced Tony D'Souza to the people of Denver and to Ann Connor, David Connor, Tom Lundstrom, Harv Bishop and many others who made it possible for Tony to regularly visit the United States and develop his ideas there. Special thanks for hospitality are due to the Xavier Center Jesuits who provided a home in Denver and supported Tony's programs. The support and encouragement of the leaders of the Bombay Jesuit province is deeply and gratefully acknowledged.

Frank Stroud, Dottie Rossi, Lynn Streeter, Catherine Bauer, Janet Dean, Harv Bishop, Denis Rodrigues, Toti Martinez, Sandra Ebling, David Connor, Vaughn Smith, Andy Bryner and Alice Levine each read the manuscript and provided thoughtful comments and criticism for which we are very grateful. Martin Wonsiewicz gave invaluable advice and encouragement based on his editorial and publishing experience. Special thanks are due to Marie Wonsiewicz who read and critiqued innumerable drafts and to Betsy Armstrong who guided us through to publication.

Finally, in awareness and gratitude, we salute the many teachers, coaches, friends and colleagues who have helped us understand life more deeply. We hope to pass their gift of awareness and understanding on to others so that we may all contribute to a society based on trust, peace and mutual understanding.

CONTENTS

EXERCISES

AUTHORS' NOTE

Why would an Indian Jesuit and a retired American high-tech executive write a book together? We collaborate because we want to distill two lifetimes of seeking into a simple practical book that all can read and put into practice. Tony has worked bringing education and better nutrition to the slum children of Mumbai (Bombay), treating the mentally ill and training young professionals. Bud has spent a lifetime building creative high-tech organizations. By using the tools we describe in this book, we have discovered a base of inner peace, strength and freedom, which helps us live simpler, more powerful lives. We find it easier to be productive. We find it easier to be happy with our lives and the world around us.

The book is based on a ten-day retreat Tony D' Souza conducted from the Jesuit Retreat House in Bandra, a suburb of Mumbai, India. Thousands have attended his retreats there, across India, and around the world. Tony's mentor and spiritual advisor for many years was Tony De Mello, author of *Awareness*, *The Way to Love*, *Sadhana*, *One Minute Nonsense* and many other well-loved books. Bud Wonsiewicz collaborated with Tony to organize and write this book. His contributions are those of a student attempting to practice these skills in everyday life. Bud is a former assistant professor of materials science at M.I.T. and a senior technical executive in the telecommunications industry.

Generally, the voice speaking should be taken as Tony's. However, both authors take full responsibility for the contents of the book.

INTRODUCTION

My brothers and sisters,
we must become what we already are.
One.

—Thomas Merton

Within each of us lives great spiritual strength. Think of Mahatma Gandhi, Martin Luther King, Nelson Mandela, and Mother Teresa. Each epitomized strength; each drew strength from resources within; each brought peace to a troubled world. Many of us seek inner peace and strength. Many of us wish to bring peace to our families, our work, our world.

We offer a practical way to tap into and grow your inner resources. The way is simple but not easy. The exercises in this book can help you develop the basic skill of awareness—a profound awareness of yourself and others. You may find yourself growing stronger every day. You may experience the inner peace that brings profound joy and liberation.

The ideas are based on ancient wisdom common to the great religions of the world. Mystics of all faiths share a common ground across faith, geography and time. Most likely, the common ground reflects our common biological heritage and evolution as humans. Our meditation techniques are similar in part because our minds and brains are similar.

The scientific understanding of the mind-brain-body connection is rapidly expanding. Various clinical studies show a connection between meditation and improved wellness, in particular a stronger immune response and relief from depression.

The practices contained in this book can help you develop the skills to cope with many of the emotional problems of everyday life with the exception of serious trauma and phobias. By increasing your awareness, that is, your ability to observe situations clearly, you gain insight into emotionally charged events. By increasing your capacity for compassion for yourself and for others, emotional conflict can be drained out of these situations. Health, both physical and emotional, is one reason to practice awareness.

Another reason to practice awareness is to develop a deeper spirituality, sometimes called mysticism. Our simple definition of mysticism is the ability to see life as it really is or, alternatively, to see ourselves as we really are. We can restate the definition from a deist vantage: Mysticism is the ability to see ourselves as God sees us.

You do not have to believe in God to practice awareness or to gain its benefits. It is not necessary or helpful to change religious or spiritual beliefs. As Thich Nhat Hahn points out, trees do better if not uprooted. If you are a Christian, you do well to use these practices to deepen your practice of Christianity. Likewise if you are a Jew, Muslim, Hindu or Buddhist, you do well to keep your roots.

Read this book with an open heart and mind, and it will draw you along the path of Truth. You will begin to see yourself as you really are rather than how you wish or fear you are. You will begin to see others in the same light, and your compassion for all will grow.

SUGGESTIONS FOR USING THIS BOOK

The exercises, which follow every chapter, are the heart of the book. They are designed to build your spiritual strength. Like many other skills, you learn about meditation and awareness by doing.

Practice, Practice, Practice.

The book is short enough to be read at a single sitting, but we don't think you will get much out of reading it that way. It is structured to serve as a guide and coach for a lifetime practice of awareness and compassion. You might try working on a chapter per week, taking plenty of time to repeat the exercises until you feel comfortable. For a more intense experience, you could follow the pace of the ten-day retreat, work on a chapter a day. Do a mid-morning and mid-afternoon meditation session.

The books format lends itself to easy use by established meditation, contemplation or prayer groups. Groups that meet weekly may wish to focus on one chapter per week and incorporate the exercise into their established practice.

As you become familiar with the exercises and the skills they build, you may want to incorporate some in your daily practice:

- Any of the Awareness exercises from Chapters 2 and 3.

- Either of the Coming Home exercises from Chapters 6 and 7.

- Using Awareness to Deal with Past Negative Experiences from Chapter 8.

If you find yourself depressed or angry, try returning to the exercises in this list. Anger and depression can be great opportunities for spiritual growth. Awareness is the tool for that growth. If I am angry with someone and blaming them for my troubles, I turn to Using Awareness to Deal with Past Negative Experiences. I usually wind up smiling or laughing within a few minutes.

You may also wish to add the recorded guided meditations appropriate for each chapter (see Appendix 1: Guided Meditations). We caution against using these guided meditations until you feel comfortable doing the awareness exercises on your own. Guided meditations are a nice addition; the exercises are essential.

Part One
BECOMING AWARE

Chapter 1
QUEST

You begin building spiritual strength by asking the basic questions: What am I looking for? Where am I going? What do I really want?

Most mornings, evenings, and often all during the day, in every city and town and in rural areas, adults, teens, and even children rush from one activity to another. Some are on foot; others are driving, and many others are using some other form of transportation, including buses, bicycles and skateboards. Young and old hurry to school, to work, to sporting events, exercise classes, after-school activities, and to shopping centers. A tide of humanity ebbs and flows. Often, I have been a part of this rush. However, on occasion I have stood at a vantage point, waiting to meet with a friend. As I watched I wondered, Where are they rushing to? What do they want? What are they looking for?

Of course, most are going about their daily routine. But are they aware of the deeper implications of the above questions: What do they really want? Where are they looking for it?

Where Do We Look for What We Want

A man is intently searching for something under a lamppost. After a while, someone passes by and asks, "Friend, what are you doing?" The man replies, "I am looking for my keys." The other man joins in the search. After about 10 minutes, the stranger asks, "Excuse me, where exactly did you lose your keys?" "I lost them over there," replies the man and continues his search. "Then why are you searching here?" persists the inquirer. "Because there is more light here."

Our institutions—our families, churches, schools and media are quick to tell us what we should want and where we should look for it. Sometimes the helpful advice works, and sometimes it doesn't. Some of us end up like the man in the story—searching for meaning in the wrong place—because the light is better there.

What do you really want in life? Where are you searching for it? How will you know when you have found it? Often, we think we are aware of these questions, and we think we know the answers. But, unfortunately, what we think we want may not be what we really want. The classic story of Siddhartha by Hermann Hesse is a vivid illustration of this human conundrum.

Siddhartha was a young man, born in a traditional Hindu family. His father was a priest in a local temple and by tradition Siddhartha was to succeed him. One day, Siddhartha begins to experience restlessness within himself. So he leaves his home in search of happiness. While on his search, he encounters a group of ascetics who live an austere life in the forest. Siddhartha is drawn to them and thinks to himself: This is what I really want. This will make me happy. He joins them and lives an austere life. He feels happy.

But after some months, the restlessness returns. Siddhartha decides to leave the ascetics and continues his search. Soon after, he meets a group of monks and is drawn to their monastic lives. He says to himself: This will make me happy. He joins them and experiences happiness. But after some months the restlessness returns. He then decides to leave the monastery and continue his search. Along his journey, he falls in love with a beautiful woman. For the first time he experiences the thrill of sexual love and says to himself: This is what I really want. He decides to stay with her. But after some time, the restlessness returns. He leaves her. Next he comes in contact with rich businessmen and he soon becomes a rich businessman himself. He has money, power and influence. He feels he has achieved what he really wanted. But the restlessness returns.

Tired of searching, Siddhartha decides to return home. Years earlier, at the start of his search for happiness, he had to cross a river. Now, years later, he is on the banks of the same river, waiting for the boatman to ferry him across the very same river. When the boatman comes near, he recognizes Siddhartha. He asks him, "Weren't you the same man who, some years ago, went across in search of happiness?" Siddhartha answers, "Yes." And then Siddhartha asks the boatman, "Have you gone across in search of happiness?" The boatman responds, "No. I am not ready yet. The river is my teacher. I am learning much from the river and I have still more to learn." Just then Siddhartha looks at the river and experiences enlightenment. He decides to be an assistant to the boatman, helping him ferry people across the river.

Let's examine the story for its essential lessons. Siddhartha, who is in touch with his restlessness, tries to deal with it by searching for happiness in one way of life after another. After many false starts he finds an end to his restlessness right where he began his search. Unlike Siddhartha, however, many of us tend to get stuck. We often relentlessly pursue what we think will make us happy. We might chase money, power, fame, status or achievement. A businessman may say to himself, "If I make a million dollars, I'll be happy." He works hard and makes a million dollars. He feels happy. But after some time, the old restlessness returns. Then he may say to himself, "Perhaps two million will make me happy." Once again, he works hard and achieves his goal. He feels happy but only for a while. The old restlessness returns. Again, he ups the ante, "Perhaps four million will make me happy."

The man, like many of us, is stuck. Instead of realizing that money fails to make him happy and that, like Siddhartha, he should search for something else, he pursues more and more of what does not really satisfy him. We witness the same phenomena in a person's struggle for power, influence or achievement.

We Look Outside for Happiness

Another important aspect of Siddhartha's story is that he looks outside for happiness.

Mr. Brown's dog, Tiger, liked to chase trucks. Whenever Tiger heard a truck on the road outside his house, he would chase it until he was exhausted and then he would return. Just when he recovered, another truck would come along and he would chase this truck, and once again, when exhausted, he would return home. Mr. White, Mr. Brown's neighbor, watched these futile efforts. One day, he remarked to Mr. Brown: "I wonder when Tiger will succeed in catching a truck." "That's not what I am concerned about," replied Mr. Brown. "I am wondering what he will do once he catches the truck."

We are like Tiger chasing trucks. We search for happiness outside ourselves. Because we are social beings, we compare ourselves with others. We all compete in a big treasure hunt, seeking wealth, power, influence or achievement. It's a race we cannot win. Someone will always have more than we do. Yet we are willing to sacrifice ourselves and climb over others in a quest for something that does not deeply satisfy us.

What We Want Is Inside

Some years ago, I met a young American woman who had traveled to India on several occasions to study yoga and meditation under distinguished teachers. She practiced many hours a day and was eager to attend more retreats with more teachers. After listening to her life story, I asked her why she was doing this. She told me that she was fed up with the materialism of the West and was now looking for the spirituality of the East. I told her that essentially she hadn't changed. She reacted strongly. "What do you mean, I haven't changed? Isn't spirituality better than materialism?" I told her that in the past she was collecting material toys to entertain herself; now she was collecting spiritual toys. The problem was that she was still collecting. Her mindset was the same. Only the object of her "treasure hunt" had changed.

The words "Don't put new wine into old wineskins" are relevant here. We need to fundamentally change our mindset. The change that is required is not just the object of our search but also our approach. Thousands of foreigners come to India in search of spirituality. Most often, the mindset is the same. Only the object has changed.

We need to acknowledge that our mindset is the result of thousands of years of conditioning. We look outside to meet our basic needs. We apply the same approach to meet our deeper spiritual needs. We need to look inside. We need a radical transformation in our way of thinking.

We think what we want is outside, but what we really want is *within* us. Kabir, the mystic poet of India, powerfully illustrates this idea. He says that the musk deer has the musk in its navel. It smells the scent but does not know the source of the musk scent. It searches for the scented object in the grass. Likewise, Kabir says, people are searching for God in temples, churches and mosques when God is in their own hearts. In another of Kabir's poems, a small fish asks the big fish: "I hear the ocean is a vast and wonderful place. Where is it?" And the big fish replies: "This is the ocean. You are in the ocean." And the small fish responds: "Oh, is that all?"

Tony De Mello tells a beautiful story expressing the same idea.

God is tired of being pestered by people asking for this and for that, so God calls a meeting of the most trusted angels and asks for suggestions as to where one can hide from pestering people. One angel advises God to hide on the highest peak of the highest mountain because no one will search there. Another angel says, "No, hide in the depth of the deepest ocean in the world and no one will search for you there."

Finally, God turns to the most trusted angel and asks: "Where do you suggest I should hide?" And the angel responds: "Hide in the human heart! No one will search for you there."

Key Points

- Inner growth begins with a profound question: What do I *really* want?
- We tend to look outside ourselves for what we think we want: money, fame, love.
- We tend to get stuck looking for what we want.
- What we want, true happiness, is inside.

A Word about the Exercise

The following exercise may give you insight into what you might be really looking for in life. Approach it with an open, expansive mind. It is not an analytical process requiring focused, rational thought. Rather, it is closer to daydreaming about a question.

Be gentle with yourself as you do this exercise. Approach it with a "no violence" attitude. Don't try to force anything to happen. Don't try to force yourself to feel or act in any particular way. Let what happens, happen.

What Do I Want?

1 Place a notepad before you and take a posture that will keep you relaxed and alert; close your eyes. Gently, ask yourself: What do I want? Let your response come from within rather than from your rational mind.

2 When you get your response, note it on your pad. After a few seconds, ask yourself: What do I really want? Again, allow the answer to surface from within.

3 When the answer comes, do not judge or evaluate it; just jot it down in your notepad.

4 Then repeat the same question: What do I really want?

5 Continue this process for about 10 minutes.

6 During the questioning process, if no answer surfaces, let it be. After a while, repeat the question to yourself. If the same response surfaces, let it be.

7 After about 10 minutes, stop the exercise, and review your responses in your notepad.

Do this exercise gently and without effort.

Chapter 2
TRUTH

Once we are aware that each of us is searching for something deep within ourselves, that what we think we want may not be what we really want, we then naturally ask: How do we move inward to find the treasure within? The answer is simple: Walk the path of truth. We invite you to follow the path of truth that leads to a new life of freedom, peace and joy.

What Is the Truth?

We know that people often disagree violently on what they consider to be the truth. Think of political opponents, quarrelling couples or religious zealots. Each is convinced that they are in sole possession of the truth. Each believes the others are out of touch with reality and are living a falsehood. Perception has become reality; the map has become the territory.

Truth *is* difficult to define. It is easier to say what it is not. Truth is not the beliefs we hold, although they may point to truth. Truth is not the conclusions we have drawn based on our experience, although they, too, may point to truth. The truth we are talking about is not the dogmas or definitive statements people make regarding religion, life, relationships and so on. It is first and foremost the truth of who we are and our place in the world.

We are not saying that belief is wrong or inconsequential. Far from it. Belief is necessary to living daily life. We are saying that the process of discovering the truth of who we truly are is lifelong and continual. This process leads to self-understanding without evaluation and judgment. Very simply, truth is what *is*: what is real. Truth is greater than our concepts or beliefs. To grow in inner strength and peace, we must be willing to go beyond our rational ideas of ourselves and the world. We must wake up and see ourselves and the world clearly. We must see things as they are, not as we believe them to be.

When we say that we will experience the truth, we are not saying we will make another belief of it. A belief is the articulation or conceptualization of an experience, however inept or inadequate it may be. Essentially, our goal is to develop the skills to directly experience ourselves, the world and others, as they actually are.

Tony De Mello's story of a conference of devils is pertinent to this idea.

The devils were sharing their successes as well as challenges in dealing with the wards entrusted to their care. They had a special way of knowing who was doing what as things were happening. During the conference, one devil said to the other, "Hey, look! Your ward has found a piece of truth." The other devil, not the least perturbed, said, "I am not worried about that. I will get him to make a belief of it."

Do You Prefer Truth or Security?

The path of truth is not so easy, as the man in the next story from Tony De Mello quickly learns.

A man noticed a shop sign. It read: Truth Shop. The man's curiosity was aroused, and he decided to enter the shop. A woman standing behind a counter welcomed him and asked, "What can I do for you, sir?" He replied, "I read that this is a truth shop. Do you sell truth?" She replied, "Yes, sir. But what kind of truth do you want? Do you want the whole truth or the partial truth?"

The man replied, "Oh! I want the whole truth." "Certainly, sir," the lady responded. "Kindly go to the other counter." The man went to the other counter and a young man asks him, "What can I do for you,

Discovering AWARENESS

sir?" The man replied, "I believe that you sell the whole truth. I want to buy the whole truth." "Certainly, sir!" the man responded, "But sir, it will cost a great deal!" "What's the price? I am ready to pay any price." The young vendor hesitatingly replied, "The price is your security." The man walked away, sad.

Often, we do not face the truth because we prefer the way we have organized our world to the truth. Being open to the truth means being open to things as they actually are, as opposed to how we believe they are. Letting go of the security we have built for ourselves from childhood can be very threatening. Think again of political opponents, quarrelling couples or religious zealots. For example, the aggrieved member of a quarreling couple often obsessively focuses on the injustices and insults they have suffered because that keeps them secure in the view that the other is at fault. The very thought of abandoning judgment of the other person's behavior undermines the fragile security and causes panic or resistance. One of the parties might ask, "Who do you think I am that I could forgive this behavior?"

Trading our security for truth is not easy, but it is essential to our progress.

A Preference for Misery?

Eric Berne, the founder of Transactional Analysis, is reported to have said that we assume when clients come for counseling or therapy, they want to change and improve. Not at all. He uses a metaphor to illustrate this behavior. It's as if people who come for therapy are in a cesspool with filthy stinking water. We would expect them to say that the water is stinking and nauseating and that they would be screaming to be pulled out of the cesspool. In fact, that is not at all what they are saying. Instead, they are saying: "Please make sure others don't make waves. It disturbs our breathing." They do not want to get out of the cesspool. They have grown comfortable with it.

We humans have very creative ways of adjusting to the worst possible situations and surviving. Consider the worst slums in the poorest countries of the world. Most people cannot imagine how anyone could survive in such misery and filth. But for the residents, life goes on. Children play and adults chat and carry on their business.

The government of Kolkata (Calcutta) wanted to help the residents of a particular slum by housing them in more comfortable and secure buildings. Each family was moved into a room in the new buildings. But after three months, they returned to the slums, which apparently were much more comfortable and secure for them. This story illustrates how difficult it is for us to change and give up the things that make us feel secure. In many cultures, social workers often complain about people not wanting to change although they are suffering greatly.

Security is very important to us. It is connected to our survival. Our drive for survival is our basic instinct. Animals and birds brought up in captivity and then released as adults tend to return to their cages because they have grown secure in captivity and have adjusted to their situation. Introducing them to a new situation, something unknown, is threatening.

When we talk of security, we are referring to two types—physical and psychological. Physical implies our bodies, our health and ultimately our life. We notice an in-built mechanism, particularly in animals, for physical survival. We humans have inherited it through the evolutionary process. However, psychological survival is peculiar to humans. When our mental concept of who we are is threatened, we experience a threat to our psychological survival. Chapter 5 covers this concept in depth. We do not like to change because we also feel threatened at the psychological level.

Change implies letting go of what has given us security and moving on to something else we think will give us security. There is a gap between what is and what will be. The gap creates fear and insecurity. It is this fear that prevents us from letting go of what we think makes us secure.

How Is Our Security Formed?

As a part of growing up, we have each received conditioning that unconsciously influences our beliefs and our behavior. Our parents conditioned us as they were conditioned. Our culture conditioned us through schools, teachers, church, social organizations and work. As we acquire discipline, good manners, taste and a sense of order, our culture passes on its traditions.

We may be proud of our punctuality, neatness, diligence, friendliness, creativity and so forth. We may believe these traits are important, even vital. Through the process of reward and punishment we develop behaviors which society considers appropriate and learn to avoid the inappropriate ones. Over time, we have managed to internalize our conditioning, and now we function almost automatically. We have organized our world and learned how to remain secure. As we will see in Chapters 4 and 5, much of this conditioning extends internally into our very sense of self and what we believe we must do to keep ourselves secure.

Compromising the Truth

When the truth we face threatens our security, we quickly find ways of compromising it. One of the coping or defense mechanisms frequently used is rationalization or justification. Through this process, we learn to cut corners. We compromise with the truth, as this Sufi story clearly shows.

Nasruddin was arrested for mixing horsemeat with chicken meat and selling it as chicken cutlets in his restaurant. He was found guilty. But before sentencing him, the judge, out of curiosity, asked Nasruddin, "Nasruddin, what proportion of horsemeat did you mix with chicken meat?" Nasruddin, under oath, promptly replied, "Fifty-fifty, your honor." He was sentenced.

When Nasruddin was released, a friend of his who was in the court when the sentencing took place, asked him, "Nasruddin, when the judge asked you what proportion of horsemeat did you mix with chicken meat, under oath you replied, 'Fifty-fifty, your honor.' What did you mean?"

Nasruddin quickly replied, "I meant one horse to one chicken."

Social psychology experiments demonstrate how subjects compromise truth to maintain psychological security, as shown in this experiment from Elliot Aronson's book *Social Animal*.

A man was hypnotized and under hypnosis, it was suggested to him that at 4 PM, he would wear his raincoat and rain shoes, take his umbrella and walk eight blocks to the supermarket where he would buy six bottles of bourbon. When he returned home, he would snap out of his hypnosis.

There are three pertinent things about the situation: (1) It is a bright, sunny day; (2) The man is a teetotaler, and does not drink alcohol; (3) A nearby store on his street sells bourbon at the same price as at the supermarket.

As per the hypnotic suggestion, the man wears his raincoat and rain shoes, takes his umbrella and walks eight blocks to the supermarket, purchases six bottles of bourbon and returns home. When he returns home, he finds himself wearing his raincoat and rain shoes, carrying an umbrella and six bottles of bourbon, having walked eight blocks to the supermarket. The experimenter questions him:

Experimenter: Where did you go?

Subject: I went to the supermarket.

Experimenter: Why did you walk all the way there?

Subject: I went to buy bourbon.

Experimenter: Why did you walk so far when alcohol is sold in the store down the street for the same price?

Subject: Well, at my age a little exercise will do me good.

Experimenter: Excuse me, why did you buy bourbon when you do not drink alcohol?

Subject: Well, you see, sometimes I get guests who like to drink, and it is good to have something handy.

Experimenter: Why are you wearing your raincoat and rain shoes and carrying an umbrella?

Subject: You know, this weather is so unpredictable. It is better to be safe than sorry.

How do we understand the behavior of the young man who was the subject of this experiment? In social psychology, there is a concept known as cognitive dissonance. We like to believe that we are normal, rational beings, like all others. When our behavior does not match or is dissonant with what is considered normal, then we experience cognitive dissonance, which threatens our sense of being normal or rational. We rationalize or justify our dissonant behaviors so that they appear more consonant with our self-concept. That is exactly what the subject in the experiment did. His reasoning makes his behaviors more plausible.

The Truth Will Set You Free

Truth is the way to life. Truth is the way to freedom. If we want to live in freedom, peace and joy, then we must choose truth over our security.

This path of truth involves being honest with ourselves—our feelings, our thoughts and our behaviors. It involves facing ourselves truthfully, although sometimes it can be very threatening and frightening. When we are able to face ourselves as we are, without evaluating or judging ourselves, then we will grow in the understanding of who we truly are. We will begin to understand why we do what we do and why we feel the way we feel. We will be able to understand where our fear originates and why we often react to certain situations more than others.

As we discover and understand ourselves, we will begin to experience greater freedom and love. We will become more compassionate toward ourselves. We will begin to feel love for ourselves and others. We will become less judgmental of others and begin to feel greater compassion for them. We will develop a deep reverence and respect for all the beings of the world, including nature. We will develop a strength and peace that nothing can change or destroy.

Discovering awareness is the key step toward truth. Our goal is to develop the skills to directly experience ourselves, the world and others as they actually are, not as we believe them to be.

Key Points

• The path of truth is to directly experience ourselves, the world and others as they actually are, not as we believe them to be.

• This path of truth involves being aware of ourselves, our feelings, our thoughts and our behaviors— without evaluation or judgment.

• To follow the path of truth, we must be willing to let go of many of the things and beliefs that make us feel secure. The price of truth is security.

• Through a process of conditioning we have developed a security system that operates automatically and mostly unconsciously.

• When truth threatens our security, we often cope by rationalizing or justifying ourselves.

• The truth will set us free.

A Word about the Exercise

Thomas Keating, the founder of the Contemplative Prayer
Movement, warns seekers not to evaluate their experiences in
meditation, offering with two observations:

- Students do not grade their own papers.
  Don't evaluate your performance in doing the
  exercises.

- The fruits of meditation are found in everyday life,
  not in the meditation itself.

Sometimes the exercise may seem easy and fun. Sometimes it
may seem hard and boring. What Keating is saying is that none of
this matters. Just keep doing the exercise; the fruits will come later.
In this way, it's much like athletic training or practicing the piano. It
isn't so important to enjoy or feel satisfied. It's just important to do it.

Here is a simple exercise to introduce you to awareness. It is
one of many exercises that focus on the simple act of breathing.
This one focuses on the sensations in your nostrils as you breathe.
It is traditionally called Anapan.

We invite you to enter this exercise with an open mind and heart.
Let the experience be soft, like the gentle rain, slowly penetrating
your thoughts and sensations.

Be gentle with yourself as you do this exercise. Approach it with
a "no violence" attitude. Don't try to force anything to happen.
Don't try to force yourself to feel or act in any particular way.
Let what happens, happen.

Awareness of the Breath

1   To begin, take a comfortable posture, one that keeps you relaxed and alert. If it helps, close your eyes.

2   Become aware of your breathing—the breath flowing in and the breath flowing out.

3   Allow the breathing to happen. If it is slow, let it be slow. If it is fast, let it be fast. If it is shallow, let your breathing be shallow. If it is deep, let it be deep.

4   Become aware of the breath flowing in. Notice the sensations in the inner walls of the nostrils as you breathe in. You might notice that more air flows through one nostril than the other.

5   Next, focus your attention on the breath flowing out. Once again, become aware of the sensations on the inner walls of the nostrils as you breathe out.

6   Now, become aware of the whole cycle of breathing— the breath flowing in and the breath flowing out. Notice the sensations on the inner walls of the nostrils as you breathe in and as you breathe out.

7   Become aware of the sensations without evaluation or judgment. Let each sensation arise and disappear in the vast spaciousness of awareness.

8   No need to control your breath. No need to control the sensations. Let the breathing happen.

9 After about 20 minutes, spend a couple of moments enjoying the silence and peace within. Then gently end this exercise.

If you find it difficult to practice for this long, you may want to start with shorter times and work up to 20 minutes gradually. When you find your attention wandering, very gently notice this. Say the word "thinking" to yourself, and return your attention to the breath. Avoid making the exercise a task or an achievement test by evaluating how well you keep your attention focused. Instead, simply and softly, return to the focus on the breath.

Use your posture to keep you relaxed and alert. Most people find a seated posture with a relaxed and erect spine to be helpful. Lying down might help you relax but won't do much for keeping you alert. Conversely, standing on one foot might keep you be alert but won't help you relax.

As before, take a "no violence" approach to the exercise. Do it gently and without effort.

Chapter 3
AWARENESS

We see now as through a glass, darkly.
— I Corinthians 13:12

If we wish to discover what we really want, then we must follow the path of truth. Awareness is the tool that will help us walk this path. It will help us to experience things as they are.

Awareness is simple to understand but difficult to practice. Awareness is the heart of spiritual growth. Its goal is simple—to see things as they are. We think we are aware. Are we?

When we see a rose in the garden, do we experience the rose directly or do we experience the memory of a rose we have in our mind? When we enjoy a dinner, do we enjoy the food or the memory of other dinners gone by? Often we do not distinguish between our experience of the present and our memories of the past. Often, the present triggers memories of the past. We live, most of the time, in a world our minds have constructed, and we are blissfully ignorant of it.

Reality is truth. However, we can't experience reality directly because we wear colored glasses. Our experience is colored by our perceptions. Our perception is filtered by our past experiences, values, attitudes and beliefs that have been developing since infancy. We are generally unconscious of how the lessons from parents, schools, organizations, etc. influence how we experience reality. So, unconsciously, we experience reality through a filter of preconceptions, beliefs and past memories.

Imagine that a close friend is coming to visit. What do you feel? If she is your close friend, you are likely to be excited. The mere news of her arrival has activated pleasant memories. The memories, rather than the present news, cause most of your excitement. This is typical. Often we experience and react to memories rather than the current reality.

Further, our mind acts as a gate to reality. Based on our values, attitudes, beliefs and past experiences, our mind evaluates the incoming reality as good or bad, right or wrong, appropriate or inappropriate. Whatever is evaluated as positive is welcomed, and whatever is evaluated as negative is pushed away.

Imagine you meet a person you strongly dislike based on your past experiences. What do you feel? Most likely you feel angry or upset even though the experiences took place many years ago. The presence of this person in the here and now activates the experience of the past stored in your brain. Are you responding to this person or are you reacting to the past event?

Elements of Awareness

Awareness consists of two elements:

- Being in the present
- Observing, without evaluation or judgment

Awareness exercises are simple to understand but difficult to do because in our everyday life we are accustomed to move instantly from a perception to an evaluation or judgment. This movement happens automatically and often unconsciously. For example, at the first taste we may declare, "This soup is delicious." Awareness asks us to observe and experience the soup and to suspend evaluation and judgment.

The elements of awareness, though distinct, are very much related to one another. Now, let us explore the elements.

Being in the Present

Buddhism reminds us that everything is impermanent and transient; everything is changing and passing. All that we have is the present moment, the NOW.

An Indian story tells of a man chased by a tiger. The man is terrified and, as he runs blindly for his life, he falls down a precipice. As he falls, he manages to grab hold of the exposed roots of a tree. He desperately hangs on. He looks up and he sees the tiger; he looks down and he sees a cobra at the bottom of the precipice. He looks at the base of the tree roots and he notices a mouse nibbling at the roots. Just above is a honeycomb. Drops of honey fall on the back of his hand. All he does is reach up and lick each drop.

The tiger is the past and the cobra is the future. As the mouse nibbles at the roots, even the present slips away. All that the man does is lick each drop of honey. This is the present moment.

Reality is only in the present. It is not in the past nor in the future. However, we find ourselves often living in the past or the future. The past is gone, never to return. The future has not yet arrived. All that we have is the present moment, which is slipping by.

We say that we are in the present. What does it mean, being in the present? When I say I am present with you, am I really? I certainly am physically present. But my mind could be somewhere else. I could be thinking of a friend who looks like you. I could be thinking of the things I plan to do after my meeting with you is over. I could be wondering if you are really interested in what I am saying or whether you like me. Being in the present means being in the now—present to what is. It involves being totally present to the reality manifesting itself here and now. In this case, it means a total absorption with you, your words and your actions, just as you are in the present moment.

Sometimes our past experiences may prevent us from being in the present. Consider a woman who was sexually abused by a tall man with dark hair when she was 10 years old. Now she is about 30. A tall man with dark hair approaches her. She reacts with fear and withdraws. Is she responding to this man or reacting to her past negative experience of the man who abused her? Obviously, she is reacting to her past. The man approaching her has done nothing to hurt her. She may not even know him. But just his presence triggers memories of her negative past and prevents her from interacting with this man.

Similarly, past positive experiences may prevent us from experiencing the present. On my first visit to the United States, I stayed in Montauk, Long Island, which is famous for its seafood. I am fond of the spicy, hot seafood dishes from my part of India and so looked forward to going out to the local restaurants for fresh seafood. When the menu arrived, I searched for something similar to my favorite dish in India. When the dish arrived, I tasted it and found it bland and disappointing. It did not have the taste I had in mind.

After about a week, I realized that I was not enjoying the lovely seafood because I was looking for something that matched the Indian dishes. So next time, I asked for the house specialty. When the dish arrived, I decided to be present to the taste of the dish without comparing it to the past memories. As I did that, I began to appreciate the delicate spices that blended beautifully with the natural taste of the fish. Slowly I began to appreciate American food and even enjoy it.

Our anxieties about the future can also prevent us from experiencing the present. We notice this in some students who are studying for exams. As they study, they worry about taking the exam. Will I remember this stuff? Will there be trick questions? Will I fail? Will I flunk out? What will my parents say? Will I ever get a job? Their worries about the future prevent them from studying in the present moment. The future blocks the present.

How much better off would these students be if they could stay in the present moment and get their work done?

Observing without Evaluation or Judgment

The second element is observation without evaluation or judgment. Observation implies neutrality and objectivity about what is being observed. This requires an emotional and psychological distance between the observer and the object observed. If we become emotionally involved with the subject, we diminish our ability to perceive reality accurately. Psychologists, when counseling or doing therapy, maintain a psychological distance between themselves and the client. This distance is necessary for the psychologist to have an objective assessment of the problem as well as the ability to empathize.

For example, in the heat of a fight we may no longer accurately hear what another is saying. If we are seized by fear, our ability to perceive the threat is impaired.

One analogy is the difference between watching a video of an emotionally charged scene and being a participant in the same scene. In the first case, we can more accurately perceive the words, actions and emotions of those involved. When we observe, we are said to be dissociated from the situation. When we are involved, we are said to be associated. Since our goal in awareness is to observe, we must dissociate from the subject of our observation.

We constantly and unconsciously evaluate our experience as good or bad, right or wrong, appropriate or inappropriate. For example, you go into a garden. You see different plants and flowers. If you observe carefully, you will find yourself evaluating or judging what you see. You are drawn to those things you evaluate as positive, and you are repulsed by those you evaluate as negative. It is difficult to observe something without evaluation or judgment. By suspending evaluation and judgment, we increase our ability to be present to reality as it is in the here and now.

The process of evaluating and judging is almost automatic. The criteria we use to evaluate something as positive or negative are values we have internalized since our infancy through our culture, institutions and experiences. This process helps us to organize and maintain order in our internal and external world. We are able to control what is happening and not be taken by surprise.

Key Points

- Awareness is the path to truth—to see things as they are.

- Awareness is

    - Being in the present

    - Observing without evaluation or judgment.

- Awareness is a skill that can be discovered and developed.

- Skill is developed by frequent practice of any of the awareness exercises.

A Word about the Exercises

The following exercises build on the experience you gained in the previous Awareness of Breath exercise. The process is the same as before; only the point of focus differs.

The first focuses on the sensations in the body; the second on the sounds that surround us. It is not the subject matter that constitutes awareness but rather being in the present while observing without evaluation or judgment.

Awareness, although a conscious process, is not strenuous. It is a conscious choosing of being in the present without violence, without denial. If awareness becomes tiring, then we are likely to be striving for awareness as a goal rather than simply being aware.

Awareness is the basic skill for spiritual strength. Practice an awareness exercise as often as you can. Your skill will increase and eventually you will find yourself living more and more of your everyday life in awareness—being in the present and observing without evaluation or judgment. You will begin to experience things as they are, not as you think they are.

Be gentle with yourself as you do this exercise. Approach it with a "no violence" attitude. Don't try to force anything to happen. Don't try to force yourself to feel or act in any particular way. Let what happens, happen.

Body Awareness

This exercise, traditionally called Vapashna, is a variation of the Awareness of Breath exercise. The method is identical except the point of focus is body sensations instead of the sensations in the inner walls of the nostrils.

1   To begin, take a comfortable posture, one that keeps you relaxed and alert. If it helps, close your eyes.

2   Become aware of any sensations at the top of your head. Slowly and smoothly turn your attention to your forehead, then the area around your eyes, then nose, mouth, chin, etc.

3   Without judgment or evaluation, notice any sensation that arises. You may notice no sensation in a part of the body. Do not be concerned. Simply continue in awareness to the next part of the body.

4   Proceed downward through your body in this manner, pausing to notice the sensations. When you reach the tips of your toes, begin the process again at the top of your head.

5   If you find yourself distracted, simply notice the distraction, say the word, "thinking" and gently shift your attention back to the body.

6   Resist the temptation to evaluate or judge your performance. Try to stay in awareness of your body and notice what happens without judgment or evaluation.

7 After about 20 minutes, spend a couple of moments enjoying the silence and peace within. Then gently end this exercise.

Take a "no violence" approach to the exercise. Do it gently and without effort.

EXERCISE
Awareness of Sounds

This exercise uses sounds as the point of focus. You may find this more difficult than the previous awareness exercises. You may notice yourself automatically evaluating or judging. If you do, just notice the judgment, and softly return your focus to the sounds.

1   To begin, take a comfortable posture, one that keeps you relaxed and alert. If it helps, close your eyes.

2   Focus on your breath for a few minutes.

3   Slowly and gently, become aware of the sounds around you—some loud, some soft; some distant, some near. They may come from all directions.

4   Be aware of each sound that presents itself to you. Do so without evaluation or judgment.

5   You do not need to identify the source of the sound; if you do automatically, let it be.

6   Sometimes, you will find yourself automatically evaluating or judging the sound; become aware of your evaluation of judgment and go beyond to observe the sound as sound.

7   If you find yourself distracted, simply notice the distraction, say the word, "thinking" and gently shift your attention back to the sounds.

8   After about 20 minutes, spend a couple of moments enjoying the silence and peace within. Then gently end this exercise.

Take a "no violence" approach to the exercise. Do it gently and without effort.

Chapter 4
FEAR

The previous chapters discussed the path to truth, which is awareness. We learned that the price of truth is our security. This brings us to the topic of fear. Fear blocks us from experiencing the truth about ourselves. We are even willing to distort the truth to avoid facing the fear.

In this chapter we examine the fear within us so that we may unblock ourselves and be free. Sometimes our fear is obvious but often it is hidden and affects almost every aspect of our lives. Exploring the dynamics of our fear will help us to understand ourselves and increase our awareness and peace.

Coming face to face with our deepest fears is a hallmark of spiritual maturity, as noted in the scriptures of the world's religions as well as in most psychological theory. Fortunately, exploring the dynamics of fear does not lead to further fear. In fact, if we explore fear with the tool of awareness our lives will become more and more "choiceful." We will be able to make choices that bring peace, joy and love. We will experience greater freedom within.

Therefore, it's crucial to understand fear in all its dimensions because fear left unchecked distorts awareness, saps strength and destroys peace, thereby affecting all aspects of our lives. We will also discover that fear is a powerful motivator, a means of controlling others and the unconscious basis for much of our behavior.

The Basics of Fear

Physical Threats

Why is fear such a strong force in our lives? At the most basic level, fear helps us survive. If fear were totally absent, we would not look before crossing the road. We might play with cobras or rattlesnakes.

Imagine a physical threat, say a tiger charging toward us, roaring and baring its fangs. A real physical threat will automatically trigger a high-speed response from our body—dilated pupils, narrowed vision, increased heart rate, fast breathing, muscles ready to fire, bladder and bowels voided. This is called the fight or flight syndrome. Unconscious and automatic systems in the brain and body prepare us instantly to run from the threat or fight off the threat. Psychologically, our response to a threat is similar to other animals and is controlled by a similar part of the brain and nervous system.

Under threat, our bodies react automatically before the rational part of the brain even realizes what's happening. The response is immediate and intense. The more primitive brain seizes control from the more evolved, rational brain. Our fear hijacks our thinking so that we can more quickly and efficiently fight or flee.

Psychological Threats

Most of the threats we experience, however, are psychological, not physical. If we perceive a great threat to our reputation, power, wealth or relationships, we experience corresponding fear. Our reputation, power, wealth and relationships, among other things, give us a sense of security. Threats to them are threats to our psychological survival.

Think of the two-year-old who constantly carries a tattered blanket. The blanket is no longer used for physical warmth but for a sense of comfort and security. What will happen if someone gently but firmly takes the blanket away? The child will react as if his or her life were threatened. It doesn't matter that the threat isn't a tiger; the child's sense of security has been threatened.

So it is with us adults. The brain does not differentiate between threat to physical survival and threats to psychological survival. It activates the fight or flight syndrome. If the threat is chronic, as in job stress or relationship stress, our body remains on constant alert with serious consequences for our physical and mental health. This is true even though there is no physical threat to our life or health. Comments like "This job is killing me" or "You make me sick" reflect the threat to our psychological survival.

To illustrate, first consider an explicit threat. Imagine a speaker giving a talk to a large audience who is interrupted by an irate member of the audience who calmly but brutally criticizes the speaker and the ideas presented. Many speakers in this situation would have a fight or flight response and react as if their physical safety were threatened. They might say afterwards, "I could have died on the spot." For some of us, a public humiliation might be a fate worse than death. Yet, what about us has been threatened? It is the sense of security, our psychological survival.

Imagine a person with mild stage fright invited to give a prestigious talk to a large audience. The mere invitation may unconsciously cause his palms to sweat and his breathing to become short. He may deny that he is afraid of giving the talk. He may make excuses and figure out a way to refuse the invitation. "I just don't like to talk to large audiences," he may say. The threat in this case exists entirely in his mind, and he is not aware of its cause or its effects. Unconsciously, something has threatened his sense of security, his sense of worth.

FEAR

Sense of Security and Worth

Many factors influence child development in a complex and interrelated way. Part of a child's sense of worth comes from the reaction of the caregivers and significant others. To the extent that care is loving and attentive, the child develops a positive sense of worth. However, no matter how loving the care may be, a child receives many different messages that influence his or her sense of worth both positively and negatively. As part of our childhood, all of us have internalized a complex set of messages about what we must do to feel worthwhile.

Conditional Messages

Beginning in childhood, we have been told things like:

• Work hard and you will be successful.

• Listen to your parents and you will be good.

Each of these messages is a conditional message. If you were to restate them as IF-THEN-ELSE logical statements, they would look something like this:

• IF {you work hard}, THEN {you will be successful}, ELSE {...}.

• IF {you listen to your parents}, THEN {you will be good}, ELSE {...}.

As children, when we comply with messages like these, we feel positive. Feeling positive about ourselves is a little reward for our good behavior and makes the behavior more likely to be repeated. When the child listens to her parents, she feels good about herself because she is a good girl. So, she is likely to listen to her parents. Over time, listening to one's parents becomes a pattern of behavior and begins to operate automatically. It also becomes part of the child's sense of worth and sense of security.

Notice the ominously dangling ELSE {…} clause. It implies negative messages that we are seldom conscious of:

- You are not successful as you are now.

- You are not good as you are now.

- So, if you do not work hard or listen to your parents, then you have no value.

If this message were presented to the child at the conscious level, she would likely experience negative feelings and fear. Negative feelings are unpleasant. Our tendency is to avoid them. But here the negative message is hidden, received unconsciously, and cannot be avoided or confronted. All the same, it affects and motivates the child. It also unconsciously threatens the child's security and causes fear.

Thus, the conditional statements contain an explicit, positive message and an implied, negative message. The first is picked up by the conscious mind; the second goes straight to the unconscious, threatens security and causes fear. In fact, it is the negative message more than the positive message that motivates the behavior, although we are usually not aware of it.

Beneath Negative Feelings Is Fear

Sometimes we are angry, jealous, anxious, worried, etc. As we gently explore our negative feelings, we may discover fear hidden beneath. Our negative feelings arise when something is threatened. When we are threatened, we experience fear. Most often, what is threatened is our sense of security or our sense of worth.

Most of the time, we are not conscious of the fear that arises from threats to our sense of security or our sense of self worth. Our socialization has very successfully taught us how to cover the insecurity and keep it hidden. We've all learned many ways to make ourselves feel secure and worthwhile.

Some of us seek security in our jobs or professions, some in our relationships, some in our wealth or possessions and some in the good opinion others hold of us. Unconsciously feeling we are not okay, we adopt a lifelong project to make ourselves worthwhile. These behaviors make us feel good and give us a sense of worth.

This pattern is so deep seated that, if we think of it at all, we tend to think of it as beliefs. I may believe that acquiring wealth is the road to happiness, or I may believe my friendships will sustain me, or I may believe that my profession is what gives life its meaning or that my reputation is my greatest asset. These beliefs cover up my unconscious fear of being nobody.

As long as the cover over the fear remains intact, we feel secure and we experience a sense of worth. However, this cover is very vulnerable and can be easily threatened.

So, the implicit, negative parts of the conditional messages of our childhood generate fear and make us feel that we have no worth, that we are not okay. We find many ways to cope with and cover up this unconscious fear.

Of course, the explicit, positive parts of the messages also create a sense of worth and well-being that is crucial to our personal development and acculturation.

Let's conclude on a non-scientific note with a Sufi story:

The mullah Nasruddin, a holy man, liked to scatter breadcrumbs all over his house. A visitor asked him why.

"To keep the tigers away," replied the mullah.

"But there aren't any tigers around here," responded the puzzled visitor.

"Exactly," smiled the mullah. "It works, doesn't it?"

Key Points

- Coming face to face with our deepest fears is a hallmark of spiritual maturity.

- Threats to our security trigger a fight or flight response that instantly affects brain and body function, temporarily overpowering the rational mind. The fight or flight response is essential for our physical survival.

- Purely psychological threats to our sense of security can produce profound fight or flight responses, even though they are not real. That is—they do not threaten our physical survival.

- Fear is a powerful motivator, a means of controlling others and the unconscious basis for much of our behavior.

- Our conditional messages in childhood make us feel we are not okay, which generates fear.

- Unconsciously, we work hard to cover up and avoid threats to our sense of security by following society's suggestions to make ourselves secure.

- Our negative feelings are flags warning us that our sense of security has been threatened.

A Word about the Exercises

The next exercises ask you to look back at the key messages you have received in life and the key people who have influenced you. Be gentle and playful with the list. There is no need to be exhaustive or to get it right. By doing this in awareness, by observing without evaluation or judgment, you may discover interesting things. Simply by bringing these finding into the light of day, they may lose their grip on your unconscious, and you find yourself more free and with more choices.

Be gentle with yourself as you do this exercise. Approach it with a "no violence" attitude. Don't try to force anything to happen. Don't try to force yourself to feel or act in any particular way. Let what happens, happen.

Messages

Recall the messages you have received in your childhood from parents, teachers and others. They may have come in different forms. If you eat all your food, you will grow strong and tall. You have done well because you have worked hard. Everyone will respect you if you are honest. If you are nice to people, they will be nice to you. List the messages below.

1	Message at the conscious level **a**
	Message at the unconscious level **b**
	Resultant behavior(s) **c**
	Feeling at the end of the behavior(s) **d**
	Ways this message is operative now **e**
2	Message at the conscious level **a**
	Message at the unconscious level **b**
	Resultant behavior(s) **c**
	Feeling at the end of the behavior(s) **d**
	Ways this message is operative now **e**

Exploring My Influences

1   Go through the various stages of your life, beginning
    from infancy, childhood and adolescence—early, middle
    and late—and list significant people in your life.

2   Next to each person, list what they valued (the values are
    expressed through their verbal and non-verbal behav-
    iors). For example, a person who constantly talks and
    worries about money it is likely to value money a lot.

3   Once you have listed the values of each person, convert
    them into beliefs. You can do that by stating (taking the
    above example): I am worthwhile if I have money.
    Convert all their values into beliefs.

4   Become aware of your life. Put a check mark next to the
    beliefs you have internalized.

5   Become aware of these beliefs control your under-
    standing of happiness.

6   Become aware of your hurts and sufferings and how
    these are linked with your beliefs.

Significant People	What They Valued	Convert into Beliefs	Internalized?

As you do this exercise, remember to be gentle with yourself and others. You don't need to be exhaustive. You can return to this exercise from time to time as you move along your spiritual path.

Part Two
COMING HOME TO
OUR TRUE SELF

Chapter 5
THE FALSE SELF

In this chapter, we will see how the fear, negative emotions, conditioned behavior and beliefs caused by our sense of insecurity are so ingrained that we develop a sense of self which some spiritual writers call the ego or false self. It is a mental image we develop to cover our fear. While it helps us to cope, it also makes us vulnerable if someone threatens our cover.

The word "ego" is commonly used in discussing spirituality. Unfortunately, it has quite contrary meanings in psychology and popular writing. So to avoid confusion, we will use the term "false self" and discuss it in terms of the previous chapters. Our goal is to use awareness to understand the dynamics of the false self and its underlying fears, as they are, so that we can choose to be who we are. As we shall see, this is easy but not simple.

Birth of the False Self

The false self is born of the fear that we are nobody. We all want to feel we are somebody. Notice the somebody-nobody theme.

In our fear, we will do nearly anything to become somebody. Our conditioning has provided us with various ways we can make ourselves somebody. We could be a doctor, we could have many friends, we could be widely respected or we could be wealthy or wise. Moreover, since our culture approves of these behaviors, we gain instant approval and reward. People begin to look up to us. However, essentially, it isn't the rewards that drive the false self. The basis of the false self is fear.

Putting this another way, the sense of worth we have developed over the years is our way of dealing with our fear of being nobody. It is as if we have built a fortress to protect ourselves from experiencing this fear. The more we fear being nobody, the more we work to become somebody.

The False Self Is an Illusion

The false self is a mental construct. In Hinduism it is called "maya," meaning illusion. We weren't born with it; it isn't part of our DNA. It's a self-built house of mirrors. In effect, we and our society have constructed this illusion on our own.

However, it seems real to us, and we take it quite seriously. We have identified with it to such an extent for so long that it has become our identity, our total reality. For an extreme example, consider the egotistical movie star who, fallen on bad times, can't get a part and so falls apart.

Since the false self is the reality of the mind, the mind plays an important role in the functioning of the false self.

The False Self Is Made of Beliefs

The mind created and sustains the false self through beliefs. If it were a building, then its beliefs would be the beams and columns. Like the columns and beams, the beliefs do not have equal importance. Some are more vital than others. If an incidental belief is threatened, the false self may shrug it off. However, if a vital belief is threatened, the false self will declare a full-blown emergency, as if a tiger were threatening its life. Our body and mind will react accordingly with a fight or flight response, since we do not distinguish between physical and psychological threats.

A simple way to express beliefs of the false self is to use one of the sentence stems: I am worthwhile if.... Or I am worthwhile because.... Some examples of the beliefs are:

- I am worthwhile if people appreciate me.

- I am worthwhile if I am promoted.

- I am worthwhile if my children love me.

We could also state our beliefs as:

- I am worthwhile because I am intelligent.

- I am worthwhile because I am successful.

- I am worthwhile because I have money, power, etc.

Threats to the False Self

Except in cases where our physical survival is threatened, whenever we experience a negative feeling, it generally means that the false self is threatened. More specifically it means that one of the beliefs of the false self is threatened. Some beliefs are simple, such as, I am somebody if I have a job. Others are elaborate and hidden, like our beliefs about what we must do to be a good parent.

When we conform to the false self's beliefs, we feel good, we feel we are somebody. If we don't conform, we feel we are nobody. We become upset, hurt or depressed.

There is another aspect to this discussion. The mind can keep the threat alive long after the cause has disappeared. For example, suppose your boss insults you in front of your colleagues. You are likely to feel hurt and upset. Your false self has been threatened. Ten minutes later he leaves the office. Will your hurt and upset vanish? No. You will think and perhaps talk about it. When you return home from work, you find yourself still upset and tense. You might even have difficulty sleeping. The whole scene of the encounter with your boss keeps replaying over and over again in your mind. The mind maintains the threat even when the cause of threat has gone. As a result, many of us live in a chronic state of fight or flight with adverse consequences to our mental and physical health.

Operating at the False Self Level

When we operate at the false self level, all our energy is involved in developing, maintaining and protecting our false self. Pursuing society's enticements is our way of developing our false self beliefs. For example, I may say that I am worthwhile if I become a manager. This will make me strive for that position. When we follow society's path, any success, no matter how small, is enough to make us feel that we are somebody. Once we have developed a particular false self belief, then our next preoccupation is to maintain it, sometimes at any cost. Good examples of this are our politicians. Once they are elected, their preoccupation is to maintain their position.

We seek recognition, appreciation and approval from others. We work hard to maintain the belief: I am worthwhile if I am successful. We seek people who will cheer us as we run along the path of becoming somebody. Like Siddhartha, in the chapter on quest, we are seeking happiness and fulfillment outside ourselves. We want the world to consider us as "somebody."

Looking outside makes us vulnerable, so we work hard to maintain our false self. If life brings us success, we try to maintain our success. Meanwhile, we realize that our success is not enough. We need more success. We compare ourselves to others. We notice that others have achieved more. Consequently, we feel badly and push ourselves harder, constantly looking over our shoulder to see how others are doing.

Finally we strive to protect success. Our sense of being somebody is brittle and can be shattered by criticism. When it happens, our tendency is to protect ourselves. We either attack those who threaten us or try to defend or justify ourselves. Sound familiar? It's the fight or flight response triggered by the false self's fear of being nobody. It's real, causes illness and suffering and blocks the path to truth.

The False Self and Suffering

We may not be able to avoid pain, but we do not have to suffer. Let us elaborate. By pain we mean a physical negative experience like a headache or toothache. Pain is a physical reality of the nervous system. However, suffering is essentially mental. Suffering comes when our false self is threatened. We feel upset, angry, irritated, depressed, lonely, jealous, etc. We may suffer because we believe we are worthwhile if, and only if, we are healthy and pain-free. Pain is a fact of life; the suffering is optional.

Conversely and paradoxically, suffering itself may lead to pain. If the false self is chronically threatened and declaring emergencies, the physical fight or flight reaction takes a toll on the body. Constant stress has been shown to lower the immune reaction and is implicated in many diseases. In the past few years, modern clinical medicine has been able to document the beneficial effect of meditation practices, such as awareness. Similarly, pain can lead to suffering. A good example is the distress a patient goes through when diagnosed with cancer. Awareness meditation can reduce the anxiety and distress, thereby helping the body fight the disease by excluding the false emergencies that the false self declares.

Dealing with the False Self

Here is the bad news. We cannot get rid of the false self. It's too ingrained and unconscious. It also isn't susceptible to a direct or violent attack.

Here is the good news. It's easy to spot the false self when it panics and, with practice, easy to loosen its grip. Our hurts and negative emotions are a giveaway that our false self is threatened. We can use our awareness skills to observe the fear and negative emotions it automatically produces. With more awareness, we can identify the belief that is threatened.

So, whenever life upsets us, we have an opportunity, courtesy of the false self, to observe our false self in action and the negative consequences it produces.

Here is how it works. Suppose someone criticizes us when we are giving a talk; we are likely to be hurt. This means that one of our beliefs is threatened. All that we have to do is ask: What do we want instead from the group? Appreciation may come up. Then the belief is: I am worthwhile if I am appreciated. This may be the belief that is threatened. Then we become aware that our survival does not depend on whether we are appreciated. Once we have done that, we can look at the criticism objectively and learn from it for the future. And so, the false self loosens its grip on us.

Sound difficult? It's easy. It just takes practice and that's what the next exercise is about.

Key Points

- Our false self or ego is a mental construct devoted to preserving a sense of self-worth.

- The false self is imaginary, consisting of unconscious beliefs about what will preserve its sense of self-worth.

- When the false self's beliefs are threatened, it reacts as if its existence were threatened. It triggers a physical fight or flight response that is instant, automatic and often unconscious. We usually notice strong negative feelings when this happens.

- We often operate under the unconscious influence of the false self, gaining a positive identity through the roles, behavior and labels we assume.

- The security gained by the false self beliefs is fragile. If we lose our role, we can lose our identity.

- We can't get rid of the false self. It's a construct of the mind, deeply ingrained and unconscious. As long as we have our minds, we'll have our false self.

- Negative feelings indicate that the false self is in control. We can use them as flags.

- Awareness practice can loosen the false self grip and provide us with real security.

A Word about the Exercise

As always, begin with a brief awareness exercise to quiet your mind and focus yourself. This exercise is particularly important as it will develop skills that will help you be resilient in the face of negative experiences. Return to this exercise whenever your feelings are hurt and you want to discover why. With practice, you will quickly identify the belief of the false self that is threatened.

Be gentle with yourself as you do this exercise. Approach it with a "no violence" attitude. Don't try to force anything to happen. Don't try to force yourself to feel or act in any particular way. Let what happens, happen.

Discovering Beliefs

- Do one of the awareness exercises: breathing, body sensations, sounds, etc. (5 minutes).

- Think of a time when you felt hurt. Ask yourself: In that situation, from that person, what did I want instead? Whatever comes up link it with the sentence stem: I am worthwhile if.... or I am worthwhile because.... This exercise will help you discover your beliefs.

- Start with the mildest negative experience. You may want to repeat this exercise until you feel skillful at tracing the path from the negative experience to the threatened belief.

- Be gentle with yourself. Avoid judgments and evaluation. Simply observe the negative experience and the belief, as it is, of itself.

Negative experience	What do I want instead?	Convert into a belief: I am worthwhile if/ because....
I feel hurt because my talk has been criticized	Appreciation	I am worthwhile if I am appreciated by the group

As before, take a "no violence" approach to the exercise. Do it gently and without effort.

Chapter 6
THE TRUE SELF

Whoever you are, no matter how lonely,
the world offers itself to your imagination,
calls to you like the wild geese, harsh and exciting—
over and over announcing your place
in the family of things.

—Mary Oliver

In the first chapter, Quest, we asked ourselves, "What do I want?" We noticed that often:

- We are unaware of what we really want, or what we think we want may not be what we really want.

- We are searching for it in the wrong place.

- We are stuck in our search.

- We have what we seek within us, but we are not conscious of it.

The previous chapters, Truth, Awareness and Fear, describe the path: The truth will set us free, awareness is the path to truth, and our fears block the path.

Through awareness, we begin to understand ourselves, as we are, without evaluation or judgment—our behaviors, thoughts, and feelings. If we practice awareness in this way, the false self described in the last chapter begins to lose its grip. We begin to see life as it is, not as we wish it to be or as we fear it is. We begin to see others and the world in the same way. We begin to enjoy our place in the family of things.

You might want to revisit the exercises in the earlier chapters before reading further.

In this chapter we reach the core and foundation of the book. Having come this far we urge you to read what follows with an open, as opposed to critical, mind and focus your efforts on the exercise Coming Home. Your personal experience from doing this exercise may make what we say here more understandable, vivid and real.

The Path to the True Self

The awareness exercises are the path to the true self. By simply observing without judgment or evaluation, we disable the false self. As we noted earlier, the false self is a reality of the mind. The role of this mind, when it is in the false self mode is to develop, maintain and protect the false self. It does this by evaluating everything that it considers useful for the false self as positive and the rest as negative. However, our awareness approach switches off this function, and as a result we are able to see things as they are.

In a sense, the false self drifts off to sleep during awareness. Without the false self saying "Yum!" or "Yuck!" we begin to see things as they are. We begin to experience the Self without any labels, symbols or concepts.

It is an experience of just being. I am. I AM.

Often as judgments, labels and distinctions disappear, words begin to fail us utterly. The failure of language is apparent in the words that different traditions use to describe this transcendent experience. Ancient Sanskrit used "*Tat Tuam Asi,*" which means "That Thou Art." It resonates with the response Moses received from the burning bush—"I am who I am." Buddhism speaks of the void that lies beyond all concepts which encompasses everything. Words fail— taste and see.

Some describe the process as a spiral journey inward from our conscious mind through the wilderness of the false self to the garden of the Self. Some compare it to peeling an onion. In awareness, we observe without evaluation or judgment each layer and move on to the next. Beneath all the layers of the false self's automatic beliefs, judgments, negative emotions and strivings, we find the Self.

We Are Perfect

The Self is who we are, just as we are—absent of any judgment or evaluation—a human, complete, whole, a masterpiece. We cannot improve upon it; we cannot deface it or take credit for it. It is just the way it is—perfect. When we experience who we truly are, we experience security within ourselves. We feel fearless just the way we are.

Unfortunately, because we tend to live in the dream world of the false self, we imagine that we are insecure and become fearful.

Wake Up!

Our task is to wake up.

The dream world of the false self can be illustrated by the image of a sleeping man.

In his sleep he dreams. He dreams that a tiger is chasing him. He runs away from the tiger. As the tiger comes closer, he runs faster and faster. He is terrified. He wakes up in a fright and looks around for the tiger. There is no tiger. He becomes aware that he was just dreaming. He laughs uncontrollably!

Now for this man the tiger is real until he wakes up. When he is asleep, he is terrified of the tiger. But when he wakes up and becomes aware, he laughs at the tiger.

Our false self is the tiger that frightens us and is the cause of our suffering. It is real to us until we wake up to the truth of who we are. When we discover our true Self, we laugh at the tiger. We realize that it is only a fiction of our mind.

Coming Home to the Self

As we practice the Coming Home exercise, we begin to discover who we truly are. We begin to see our place in the family of things. This just IS. It is reality. Think of a cat reclining on a sunny windowsill, perfectly content, perfectly aware and perfectly ready to act, yet at rest.

We share the same ground of being with the cat. Nothing we do, or don't do, can change our Self. Whether or not we are aware, whether or not we meditate, we simply are. I AM. It is a given and we can do nothing about it.

The only question is are we dreaming or awake? Are we aware or not?

Key Points

- As we lull the false self to sleep by suspending judgment and evaluation, we begin to glimpse and wake up to the core of our being, the true Self.

- Each of us has intrinsic worth. This is the true Self.

- The Self is who we are, just as we are, absent of any judgment or evaluation—a human, complete, whole, a masterpiece.

- We share this ground of being with all other living things.

A Word about the Exercise

The next exercise offers a path to experience a bit of the true Self. It is perhaps the most important exercise in this book and the most difficult to begin because our false self will resist and raise a number of questions. It also offers the most immediate sense of well-being.

The exercise also appears ridiculous. That's our conscious mind talking. It may even be our false self talking. Just ignore that voice and plunge in using the awareness skills you've been practicing. If you practice this without evaluation or judgment, it should slowly have its intended effect, which is to bypass the false self and let the shy, retiring Self emerge from the shadows and into the soft light of awareness.

The exercise will let the truth about yourself seep in, and slowly you will begin to relish the experience and feel at home with who you are. You savor the truth about yourself. You are like a pauper who suddenly inherits a billion dollars.

With practice, it will become easier and faster to put the false self to sleep and let the Self emerge. As your skill builds, you may be able to call on the exercise at a moment's notice and experience its calming and strengthening effect in seconds.

Be gentle with yourself as you do this exercise. Approach it with a "no violence" attitude. Don't try to force anything to happen. Don't try to force yourself to feel or act in any particular way. Let what happens, happen.

You should repeat this exercise often. Make it a part of your daily practice.

EXERCISE
Coming Home A—
Experiencing Myself as I Am

1   Do one of the awareness exercises: breathing, body sensations, sounds, etc. (5 minutes).

2   Pick one of the following sentences or phrases that appeals to you:

    a   I am complete ... I am whole ... nothing to be added ... nothing to be deleted ... just perfect ... just as I am ...

    b   All I can do is just be ...

    c   I cannot improve myself ... I cannot discredit myself ... I cannot take credit for who I am ...

    d   I am worthwhile ... somebody ... just as I am ...

    e   I just enjoy my being ... my fullness ...

    f   I am good ... loveable ... holy ... just as I am ...

    g   I am God's masterpiece ...unique ... only one ... precious ...

    h   am created ... in the image ... and likeness ... of God ...

3   Say the statement to yourself consciously (conscious of the meaning of what you say and its emotional impact on you), even though you find it difficult to believe or accept. Allow yourself to feel what you are saying.

4 Repeat it slowly but with full consciousness of what you are saying. You may say it with the rhythm of your breathing.

5 Gradually allow the sentence to shorten itself into a phrase like, I am God's image ...God's likeness ...like God ... Let the shortening happen spontaneously.

6 Savor the truth of the phrase until you are satisfied. If you wish, select another phrase or sentence. Follow the same approach. Remain with the sentence that appeals to you.

Caution: Avoid making this exercise intellectual and analytical even though such thoughts will surface. Take a "no violence" approach to the exercise. Do it gently and without effort.

Chapter 7
THE LARGER SELF

As we practice, our false self's grip diminishes, and we become more aware of our true nature, our true Self. We may have sensed that our Self is grounded and intimately joined with the larger SELF that permeates all reality. This chapter recapitulates the structure, explores the SELF, and concludes with another version of the Coming Home exercise.

Please read with an open, non-critical mind, and focus on the exercise. It speaks louder than words.

False Self

False self is an illusion we have created in our mind. Fearing that we are nobody and worthless, our false self labors to make us somebody and worthwhile. Society provides many roles and structures to help this effort. Over the years, we have developed our self-worth by acquiring knowledge, power, position, status, influence, wealth, etc. As long as these remain intact, we feel secure. However, when any one of them is threatened, then the insecurity is exposed and fear will surface. We quickly react with fight or flight response, as if our physical survival is threatened.

All our suffering comes from the false self. We make a distinction between pain and suffering. Suffering is mental and pain is physical. Whenever we experience a negative feeling it is an indication that our false self is threatened. At the false self level, we are very vulnerable because the many things that we think make us worthwhile can be threatened or lost.

Our negative feelings are the flags that warns us that our false self is threatened. The Discovering Beliefs exercise (Chapter 5) is our means for gaining an awareness of the role of the false self and its beliefs.

True Self

Our true nature is the Self. We are worthwhile, just as we are. We have a place in the family of things. We are good, lovable and holy just as we are.

When we begin to live at the Self level, we experience the security of who we are. We become fearless because nothing can change this reality. When we live at the Self level there is no suffering. When there is nothing to lose, there is nothing to fear.

The Coming Home exercises in this and the previous chapter are our means for experiencing the true Self in a way that is beyond rational thought.

The Larger SELF

As we begin to rest and relax in our true Self, we may realize that our Self is grounded in a larger reality that we call SELF. When we experience this hidden ground of our being, we gain another perspective to reality. Everything is suffused with the presence of the divine. Thomas Merton calls this "the Hidden Ground of Love." Others call it God, Great Spirit, Higher Power, Nature, the Void. The important thing to remember is that the reality transcends all words and all concepts. Literally, words fail us.

Mystics have used different images to express the same experience. Some have said that it is like a drop (Self) merging into an ocean (SELF). In Hindu scriptures the image is Atman (Self) and Brahman (SELF). Christians speak of the Christ within. Buddhists speak of our

Buddha Nature. We will use the term Self/SELF to denote this merging or grounding of Self with SELF.

In other words, we are, by our very nature, in union with the divine, the union pointed to by the term Self/SELF. Since unity with the divine is the hallmark of a mystic, we are by our very nature mystics. There is no need to become a mystic. We only need to discover our mystic nature.

Equivalently, we can use secular language to describe this experience. As we begin to see ourselves as we really are, and to see others and life in the same way, we may realize a profound interrelationship between all things. This gives us another perspective on reality that Thich Nhat Hahn calls *interbeing*. The common ground that all things share leads us to an understanding and love that we experience as compassion so deep that it surpasses our language and concepts. This is a secular description of a mystic.

Tony De Mello gives us this story to illustrate how limited our perception of the transcendent is.

A saint was once given the gift of speaking the language of the ants. He approached one, who seemed the scholarly type, and asked, "What is the Almighty like? Is he in any way similar to the ant?"

The scholar said, "The Almighty? Certainly not! We ants, you see, have only one sting. But the Almighty, he has two!"

Key Points

- Experiencing the true Self, glimpsing ourselves as we really are, often leads to a sense of connection to everyone and everything.

- We refer to this common ground of all beings as the larger SELF.

- Mystics throughout the ages and throughout the world struggle to express this experience.

- In a spiritual and mystic sense, this is what we mean by the SELF.

A Word about the Exercise

Spirituality is to discover who we really are. It is a process of coming home—coming home to our true nature. The exercise that follows is a variation of the Coming Home exercise in Chapter 6. It may help you glimpse the union of Self/SELF.

Be gentle with yourself as you do this exercise. Approach it with a "no violence" attitude. Don't try to force anything to happen. Don't try to force yourself to feel or act in any particular way. Let what happens, happen.

EXERCISE
Coming Home B—
Experiencing Myself as I Am

1 Use the method of the Coming Home exercise in
Chapter 6 to savor the following sentences:

- God loves me because He/She ENJOYS loving me.

- He/She loves me because He/She sees His/Her OWN
  IMAGE AND LIKENESS in me and not out of pity or
  as a favor.

- He/She does not expect anything in return.

- Perhaps, one expectation: He/She would like me to
  ENJOY His/Her Love.

- He/She leaves me free to return His/Her love.
  His/Her love is not contingent on my love for
  Him/Her.

2 Recall the times when you felt happy the way you
are…not for what you did…or what you achieved…just
the way you are. Relive each of those times and savor
the experience. (Reliving means going through the
experience as if it is happening to you right now.)

3 Recall the times when others loved you just the way you
are. Relive each of those times.

4 Recall experiences you have had of the Divine and re-
experience how you felt about yourself each of those times.

Do this exercise gently and without effort.

Chapter 8

A PSYCHOSPIRITUAL FRAMEWORK

"Name one practical, down-to-earth effect of spirituality," said the skeptic who was ready for an argument.

"Here's one," said the Master. "When someone offends you, you can raise your spirits to heights where offenses cannot reach. "

—Tony De Mello

The next step on our journey pulls together the psychological and spiritual concepts of the preceding chapters and places them in a simple framework. We look back to the creation story that has influenced the western world's view of human nature and examine it from the perspective of the previous chapters. From this viewpoint, a new understanding and approach to spirituality emerges. The chapter concludes with the exercise, Using Awareness to Deal with Past Negative Experiences. We hope you will find it a valuable tool.

This is a key exercise because our resilience in the face of negative events is a measure of our spiritual peace, strength and freedom.

The Psychospiritual Framework

Let us summarize what we have discussed in the previous chapters:

True Self

- We are worthwhile just as we are.

False Self

- The false self is based on the unconscious fear that we are nobody and worthless.

- The fear motivates us to make ourselves somebody and worthwhile.

- When we are very young, our false self arises from the fear generated by the conditional messages we received.

- Our efforts to make ourselves somebody reinforce the implied, negative message—We are nobody.

- The implications of the above reasoning are that we need to discover and become aware of who we truly are.

Awareness

- Awareness is the tool that will help us to see ourselves as we truly are and operate from that level.

- The path of awareness and truth leads us to the true Self.

- Awareness also helps us understand the operation of our false self.

- When we operate at the Self level, we are secure just as we are.

- When we operate at the level of the false self, we are vulnerable. Despite our efforts to cope with or hide the fear, our fortress walls are easily breached. Our negative experiences are the evidence of this breach.

What Does It Mean to Be Created in God's Image?

It's instructive to view the creation account of Genesis in the light of this psychospiritual framework. We do so not to draw you towards a particular religious tradition but to share how what we have said so far is echoed in our tradition. We are sure you will find similar stories in your own tradition. For us, the story ties things together. If you wish, you can skip this section.

Although detailed scholarly interpretation is beyond the scope of this book, we note that the authors of Genesis brought together a complex web of prior stories and traditions. Here we look at the story through the filter of the psychospiritual framework.

In the first chapter of Genesis, we read:

God created man in his image; in the divine image he created him; male and female he created them.

This implies something about our intrinsic nature. In our traditional religious practice we tend to ascribe to God certain attributes. We could say that God is goodness, love, holiness. And if we are created in the image and likeness of God then we are good, lovable and holy just as we are. This is our true identity. We are worthwhile just as we are. We take this as a description of the true Self/SELF.

When we summarize the temptation story, we discover a number of conditional messages.

The moment you eat of it your eyes will be opened
implying your eyes are closed
and you will be like gods
implying you are not like gods
Who know what is good and what is bad
implying you do not know what is good and bad.
The woman saw that the tree was good for food, pleasing to the eyes and

desirable for gaining wisdom

the conditional conscious message is positive and therefore attractive.

So she took some of its fruit and ate it; and she also gave some to her husband, who was with her, and he ate it

resultant behavior.

We have noted earlier that all conditional messages have implied negative messages that affect us unconsciously. We note that the snake's message has an implied negative component:

You are not like God. But if you eat the fruit, you will become like God.

Or alternatively, *You are nobody. But if you eat the fruit you will become somebody.*

In the words we have been using, the message is that you are not complete as you are. This understanding corresponds closely to a threat to the false self.

Like Adam and Eve, most of us at this point take the snake's bait and swallow the implied message: You are not like God. You are incomplete; you have a lot of shortcomings. Do something and you will be a better person. We then work constantly to make ourselves as good and as lovable as possible. We teach our children to do the same by offering them conditional messages on how to make themselves better. Our misguided efforts to improve ourselves and our children result in the birth of our false selves, whereas our birthright is our true Self.

In this story, humans are created with intrinsic dignity and worth. Like a cat basking in the sun, no work is necessary for us to be good, loveable and worthwhile. We just don't know who we really are.

Spirituality:
A New Understanding
and a New Approach

The psychospiritual framework offered radically changes our understanding of spirituality. Spirituality is not a method of *becoming* good, lovable and holy. Spirituality is a method of *discovering* who we truly are—good, lovable and holy, our true Self. By using the tool of awareness we can help ourselves experience our true Self and free ourselves from the clutches of the false self.

Spirituality is the art of seeing yourself through God's eyes. You perceive yourself as God perceives you, understand and accept yourself as God accepts you and love yourself as God loves you. Equivalently, spirituality is the art of seeing yourself as you really are and others as they really are. You understand and accept and love yourself as you are.

Another way of understanding the discovery of the true Self through the process of awareness is by this fanciful analogy that distinguishes between a builder and a sculptor.

- A builder constructs a structure to fill an empty space.

- A sculptor glimpses a figure hidden in a block of stone and chips off pieces until the image emerges.

The builder's process is an analog of how the false self develops. The false self senses unconscious needs and fills it by building a structure of conditioning and beliefs to make things workable and safe.

The sculptor's process is an analog of how awareness leads us to the Self and the SELF. In awareness, we sense the Self within. Awareness chips off the superfluous conditioning and beliefs so that the Self/SELF may emerge.

Discovering the Self is not an event but a life-long process of living in awareness. When we are not aware, we automatically switch to the false self. When we are aware, we can choose to be at the Self level and through that experience freedom and joy.

When we come home to our true Self, our perspectives change. We begin to see ourselves with compassionate eyes. We begin to understand, accept and love ourselves. We begin to see others with compassion and, as a natural consequence, we begin to understand, accept and love others. We begin to see that we are a seamless part of "the family of things" referred to in Mary Oliver's poem quoted at the beginning of Chapter 6. We may glimpse the hidden ground of all being, the SELF.

Love and Nonviolence Happen

It would seem that to be aware and loving all the time would take a superhuman effort. In fact, if we force ourselves we will become exhausted and fail, which is why some seekers become tired, driven and unhappy. Their false self is trying to do all the work all by itself. There is an easier way. If you can put your false self to sleep, awareness and love will happen effortlessly. The more you practice the exercises in this book, the better you will become at putting the false self to sleep. The method is simple—observe without evaluation or judgment. Soon the skill can be accessed effortlessly when needed.

When we are at the Self level, most of the things we have tried to acquire through religion and other spiritual practices will start happening. Love becomes the basis of our lives. Love flows through us in the form of caring, understanding, acceptance and forgiveness. We become slow to judge or evaluate. We experience compassion. Compassion is love with understanding. We experience peace within, not a graveyard peace that is the result of burying our conflicts but a genuine peace that is not dependent on the situation outside. If we have been raised in a religious tradition, we begin to find new depth and beauty in that tradition.

Being at the Self level also leads us to a life of nonviolence. We become nonviolent toward ourselves and others. We begin to see others as operating from love or fear. When we see someone operating from fear, we feel compassion for the person. It becomes easier for us to understand and accept people with different social and cultural backgrounds. We can more easily see other people's perspectives. We become slow to judge or evaluate. Nonviolence becomes a way of life. Mahatma Gandhi, who experienced this effect as a result of his spirituality, said, "We must become the change we want to see in the world."

Enjoying Nature and Freedom

In addition to experiencing love and nonviolence, we begin to enjoy life more and more. We are able to be present at whatever we do without evaluation or judgment. We are able to see things as they are. We begin to enjoy nature. In the company of nature we are drawn more and more in communion with all that is.

Nature is always true to itself and operates from within. When a tree bears fruit, it does not look around to see if there is anyone to enjoy it. When a flower releases its fragrance, it does not see if there are people to enjoy its beauty and fragrance. It is in the nature of the tree to bear fruit and in the nature of the flower to release its fragrance. In other words, when nature is true to itself, its fruit happens.

Freeing ourselves from the false self's attachments, we experience greater freedom from within and greater joy in life. Tony De Mello notes, "When a bee is stuck to the honey, it cannot enjoy honey. It has to be free from the honey to enjoy it." Similarly, when we are attached or addicted to something or someone, we cannot enjoy it. In short, it is only at the Self level that we can truly enjoy life and freedom.

The false self traps us in the fear of being nobody and losing many things that make us somebody. When we experience fear because our false self is threatened, we react automatically. However, when we are at the Self level, there is no fear, only love. Then we are likely to respond to a situation rather than react automatically. At the Self level, our lives become filled with choices. We see the various options and choose those that we consider most appropriate in the given situation.

Key Points

- We are worthwhile just as we are.
  This is our true Self.

- Unaware of this, our false self tries to make us worthwhile by means of a system of unconscious beliefs based on conditional messages. "You are worthwhile, if … ."

- Inner peace, strength and freedom depends on us discovering our true Self and, as a result, slowly letting go of our false self. True spirituality is a process of discovering who we truly are.

- For us, spirituality is to see ourselves as we truly are and to see others as they truly are. In theistic terms, to see ourselves through God's eyes and as a result we begin to see others as God sees them. It is a process of discovering rather than becoming.

- The path of discovery is to slowly, piece by piece, loosen the hold of the false self through the tools of awareness.

- As awareness loosens the grip of the false self and its beliefs, our perspective changes. We begin to see ourselves and others without judging. Love and non-violence begin to happen. We begin to have a deeper experience of harmony with nature and greater inner freedom.

A Word about the Exercise

So far on your journey, we hope you have found the exercises as valuable as the text. Please make sure you feel comfortable with one of the Coming Home exercises before proceeding. These exercises are the foundation.

In the next exercise, we invite you to gently examine your past negative experiences from the security of the Self. You may find this a useful skill that leads to more peace and freedom in your everyday life.

Be gentle with yourself as you do this exercise. Approach it with a "no violence" attitude. Don't try to force anything to happen. Don't try to force yourself to feel or act in any particular way. Let what happens, happen.

Using Awareness to Deal with
Past Negative Experiences

1 Make a list of past or present negative experiences that are affecting you now.

2 Select one experience from the list you've just made. If you are doing this exercise for the first time, then take the mildest negative experience. Identify the ego belief that is being threatened in this experience.

3 Do one of the awareness exercises: breathing, body sensations, sounds, etc. (5 minutes).

4 Do one of the Coming Home exercises. Feel that you are worthwhile just as you are (5 minutes).

5 From the security of Self, become aware of the negative experience you selected.

  a Watch the incident taking place; observe the sequence.

  b Listen to the words exchanged.

  c Watch the behaviors—yours and the others involved.

  d Watch the emotions that are in you and others out there.

Continue feeling secure in who you are. (If you feel any negative feelings while doing step 5, go back to step 4 and then proceed to step 6.)

6 As you go through this step, always remain secure in the Self and maintain a distance between the Self and the false self (negative experience). The image for this step is sitting on the bank of the river (security of Self) and watching the river flow (negative experience). Become aware that in the negative experience:

a Your false self is feeling threatened. (The negative feelings will give a clue regarding the fear that is operating and behind the negative feelings.)

b Your beliefs are being threatened. (Beliefs are stated as: I am worthwhile if/because …)

c Reaffirm to yourself that your worth is not in what the belief indicates but in who you are... the Self.

d The false self has taken the belief seriously and now the false self is trying to protect or defend itself from a threat that exists only in the mind.

e The false self has taken you for a ride. (Recall the image of how the tiger in the dream created havoc until the dreamer woke up.)

Note: If at any time during this step you experience negative feelings, it means that you have identified with the negative experience and with the false self. (You have jumped into the river.) You should then do the Coming Home exercise you chose in step 4 and when you feel secure at the Self level (climb onto the bank of the river), do step 6 (becoming aware of how the false self is present in the negative experience).

When the exercise is done properly, you might find the whole

A PSYCHOSPIRITUAL FRAMEWORK

situation humorous, small and insignificant. You can more easily admit if there is some problem regarding your own behavior or you understand the other person better. The negative feelings totally disappear.

7   Now go back in fantasy to the negative situation and deal with it from the perspective of the Self. Notice the difference. Become aware of the freedom and "choicefulness" you experience.

Take a "no violence" approach to the exercise. Do it gently and without effort.

Part Three
APPLICATIONS TO EVERYDAY LIFE

Chapter 9

PERSON AND BEHAVIOR

A harsh, judgmental attitude narrows the vision, saps the spirit and makes life difficult. We gain strength when we learn the skill of seeing clearly without constant criticism. Seeing ourselves and others clearly, we replace judgment with compassion and fear with love.

This chapter builds on the skills of the Coming Home and Awareness exercises to help us drop judgmental attitudes toward others and ourselves. This does not mean that we blindly accept the unacceptable. It means that we clearly distinguish between the person and the behavior. It means that we become aware of the criteria we use and how they were formed. We learn to observe without judgment or evaluation so that we may see clearly what happened. We learn to apply our criteria to the behavior not to the person. We refuse to allow our own person to be defined by another's evaluation. We recognize our intrinsic worth. We see the intrinsic worth of others. As we become less critical and judgmental, we grow in compassion and love. We begin by separating person and behavior.

Separating Person and Behavior

We make a distinction here between

- *person,* referring to who one is, namely the true Self,

and

- *behavior,* meaning the way in which one acts or conducts oneself, especially towards others.

We often confuse, confound and conflate person and behavior.

He is lazy. She is intelligent. Closer to home we may think of ourselves in terms of the labels others give us. I am strong. I am shy.

Notice the verb in all of these statements. It's the verb to be. The verb equates person and behavior as follows:

- He = lazy.

- She = intelligent.

- I = strong.

- I = shy.

By mistakenly equating person and behavior, people tend to evaluate the person by their behavior.

- If the behavior is judged positively, then the person is good and receives a positive label.

- If the behavior is judged negatively, then the person is bad and receives a negative label.

We also implicitly assume that:

- If the person is good, then the behaviors will be good.

- If the person is bad, then behaviors will be bad.

Common and deep-seated as these notions are, they are serious errors. The person and the behavior are separate. The person's worth is intrinsic. Given different contexts, the behavior can be judged as either good or bad. We cannot improve the person but we can modify or change or improve the behavior so that it fits a particular context.

Person

Each individual is a person with intrinsic worth, which we have called the Self. We cannot improve upon our Self, nor take credit for our Self. Who we are is not our behavior. We are each a masterpiece. We are unique and precious, just as we are. This means as persons we are all equal. These ideas find resonance in the secular declarations, "the inherent dignity of all individuals" or "all men are created equal."

If you are experiencing trouble at this point, please stop and return to one of the Coming Home exercises. The exercises provide a direct, personal experience to the Self that we are laboring to describe in words. Repeat Coming Home until you feel comfortable. It's the foundation.

Discomfort from doing the Coming Home exercises is often something like this, What do you mean, "Perfect, just as I am?" I'm anything but perfect. Fair enough. However, as we begin to clearly distinguish our behavior, which is anything but perfect, from our person, which is our Self, our experience changes.

Behavior

Behavior is what we do, not who we are. Behavior can be judged as good or bad, right or wrong, appropriate or inappropriate depending on the context or situation. Notice the judgment and evaluation of the behavior in this process. We need clarity on what's the behavior and what's the judgment.

How can we distinguish between the behavior and the judgment? We need to develop our skill—learn to observe without judgment or evaluation. Sound familiar? It's exactly the awareness skills we have been developing all along but applied to behavior rather than breathing.

Because judging is so automatic and unconscious, making the distinction takes practice in awareness, awareness, awareness.

An Analogy— Video Camera Language

An analogy with what a video camera sees and hears may help clarify. A video camera picks up behaviors—verbal and nonverbal—it makes no evaluation or judgment.

Consider the statement, You ignored me yesterday. Is this an observation or a judgment of behavior?

Can being ignored be seen by the video camera? No, it can't. It only sees the other person passing by without saying anything. Thus, ignoring is not a behavior but a judgment of the behavior of passing by without saying anything. By using video camera language we can choose to make a cleaner and more precise statement, When you passed me yesterday and didn't say anything, I felt ignored. Of course, by then, you may have collapsed in laughter at your leap to judgment and decide to ignore the whole thing.

What Behavior Is Appropriate and Inappropriate?

On what basis do we evaluate behaviors? In our mind we have a set of criteria by which we judge behaviors. The criteria determine which behaviors are considered appropriate in a particular culture, particular context and particular situation. They help us to do what is considered "proper" in a particular context.

Origin of Criteria

How do we judge what's appropriate? In most cases what is appropriate or inappropriate seems self-evident. However, if we probe more deeply, the judgment is made on the basis of criteria that we have acquired through the process of socialization. They are often unconscious and that's why it seems self-evident to us.

As long as the criteria remain unconscious, it is difficult to change our attitude toward certain behaviors. This tends to make us rigid and closed to people or cultures different from ours.

Cultural Context

A behavior considered appropriate in one culture may be considered inappropriate in another. For example, belching is considered extremely bad manners in western culture. However, elsewhere it is a way of expressing one's gratitude and enjoyment of the meal.

So, the society sets up behavioral criteria. Behaviors adopted by the majority, over a period of time, become the norm. Minorities within the society who behave differently are considered abnormal. For example, in rural India a right-handed person is considered normal because a majority of people are right-handed. Left-handed people are considered abnormal.

Some years ago, I was invited to conduct a program for teachers in Ooti, Tamil Nadu. I was asked to take a three-wheeler to the convent and pay the driver 20 rupees. When I reached the convent, I pulled out my wallet and offered the man 20 rupees. He said something in Tamil which I did not understand and refused to take money. I thought he was demanding more money. So, I argued with him saying that he had agreed to 20 rupees. The conversation went on for a while. Then he used a word, which in Tulu language, which I know, means hand. I looked at my hand and realized that I was holding the money in my left hand. I shifted it to my right and handed it over to him. He gladly accepted the money and left. In his culture, handing over things with the left hand is considered an ill omen.

The English language has the residue of a similar attitude in the words sinister, gauche and left-handed compliment. Our prejudices are rooted in these unconscious criteria.

Bondage of Criteria

Culture-specific criteria form a part of our value system. They underpin many of our false self beliefs and our expectations of others and ourselves. These criteria help us feel secure in the complex world around us. If others operate within the norms or criteria, we are comfortable. However, when we encounter behaviors that do not fit our criteria we feel upset. We may demand that the other person change: Stop it! We may avoid people: Not my kind of person. Prejudice flows from these primitive, unconscious beliefs and expectations. The path of prejudice leads to discrimination, violence, warfare and genocide.

The same is true of our own behavior. We may become hard on ourselves demanding instant and violent change. Or we become depressed so we can avoid the issue entirely. This path ends in self-destruction and suicide.

However, all of us need criteria to operate in society. Our goal is to become aware. We seek to hold our criteria in a gentle, open hand rather than in a tight and rigid fist.

Key Points

- Our person has intrinsic dignity and worth. It is our true Self. The worth does not depend on how we behave or how we or others judge us.

- Our behavior can be observed without judgment or evaluation. This is what a video camera does. Capturing what is. Nothing more, nothing less.

- Judgments of our behavior are based on the criteria that are usually determined by our society. They can be useful or the source of prejudice, discrimination and violence.

- A critical skill in awareness is to clearly distinguish between the person (who always has dignity) and the behavior (which may be judged as good or bad).

- Exercises can help us build our awareness skills so that the distinction between person and behavior is natural, quick and effective.

A Word about the Exercises

These two exercises take a slightly different approach than the exercise in Chapter 8. Give them a try with easier situations first, then work on more troubling ones. If you find yourself becoming upset, stop, use the Coming Home exercises and try again. Once again, the skills you learn here will serve you well in coping with stressful negative situations.

Be gentle with yourself as you do this exercise. Approach it with a "no violence" attitude. Don't try to force anything to happen. Don't try to force yourself to feel or act in any particular way. Let what happens, happen.

EXERCISE
Separating Behavior and Judgment

1   Choose a situation when you felt someone was unfair
to you.

2   Write down exactly how you felt about it without
censoring your words or language.

3   Once you have finished expressing what you felt about
the incident, go over what you wrote and underline
evaluations and judgments that you pick up, using the
technique of video language to identify the judgments.

4   Now go over the underlined judgments, one by one, and
above each convert the judgments into behaviors. For
example, instead of saying, She upset me, write, She said,
'You are so insensitive,' and I felt upset. Transform each of
the underlined judgments into behavioral terms that a
video camera could record.

5   Now read the whole account again but this time instead
of reading the judgments, read the behavioral statements.

6   Notice how you feel about the situation.

Take a "no violence" approach to the exercise. Do it gently and
without effort.

Exploring Our Criteria

In the first column, make a list of behaviors that you do not like in yourself and in others. In the second column, identify the criterion that is used to evaluate it negatively. In the third column, challenge the criterion by asking, What is so sacred or special about this criterion? Do this for each of the sentences.

With this exercise you not only make your criteria conscious but you reduce their absolute, automatic power.

A Behavior I Don't Like in Myself	Criterion for the Behavior	Challenge the Criterion
I sleep until 9 and my mother considers me lazy.	Early risers are better than late sleepers. They get more done and lead fuller lives.	If I get my share of the work done and lead a full life, what does it matter if I sleep later than others?

Take a "no violence" approach to the exercise. Do it gently and without effort.

Chapter 10
LABELS, ROLES AND IDENTITY

We hope the previous exercises have helped you discover some interesting distinctions between you and your behavior and that you have been able to extend that to others and their behavior.

All of us use a kind of unconscious shorthand in describing people. We use labels, such as lazy, athletic or trustworthy, and we understand roles, such as physician, teacher or policeman. The shorthand of labels and roles serves a critical function in the day-to-day operation of society, as in the directive, "Seek help from a physician immediately." We recognize immediately what to do, although we may be clueless about the identity of the physician.

From our perspective, the problems arise when we confuse our labels or roles with our identity. We may seek to enhance our sense of self-worth by identifying with a role. We may find our identity threatened by a threat to our role. Or we may judge others by their labels or roles. Spending some time increasing our awareness of this process may pay big dividends. When we see ourselves and others more clearly, we usually become more compassionate and more secure. As a consequence, many everyday problems evaporate without us doing anything but being aware.

Seeking Identity through Behavior

Consciously or not, most of us seek to enhance our identity through our behavior. The roles we assume are in effect sets of behaviors. Frequently, we automatically identify ourselves with our professions, which are our roles. For example, if someone asks you,

"What are you?" you might say, "I am a doctor." Or you might say, "I'm a Buddhist, or a runner, or a conservative." Thus, we seek roles that are highly valued in our society and thereby develop our false self. The false self believes, I am worthwhile, because I am a doctor.

Although the identity furnished by our role makes our false self feel good and more secure, it also makes us vulnerable. If someone criticizes us, we take it personally because we do not separate the person we are from the role we have. Or if we lose our role and are fired or demoted, we may feel as if we are nobody. In our example, the same may be true of a doctor who retires. After a few months, she may consider herself a nobody. Life may seem barren and meaningless because her worth depended on the role of being a doctor. Our intrinsic value, however, is not conditional on either our behaviors or our roles. Happy are those who retire knowing that. They have come home.

We may also mistakenly value other people because of the role they play in society and the value placed on that role. We may say, "Mary is a school principal," implying, therefore, that she is a good person." In our eyes, Mary's worth is enhanced by her role.

Violating Our Person

We often unconsciously allow others to violate our person. When someone says, "You are lazy," that person judges our behavior and equates it to our person. When we hear a statement like this, we are likely to experience a threat to our false self and immediately react with a denial, a challenge, a threat or a defense. In doing so, we tacitly accept the equation, You = lazy as the basis for action or discussion.

There are ways in which we can respond to avoid the violation of our person. If my mother says to me, "You are lazy," I can use the skills developed in the preceding exercises to separate my person from my behavior. For example, I could say to myself, "I am a wonderful person. My mother considers my behavior of getting at up 9 instead of 6 as lazy." If I develop the skill of separating person and behavior, I can prevent the violation of my person.

Once I have separated person and behavior, I am able to look at the behavior more objectively and check to see if there is some truth in what my mother has said. If I am not able to see the truth in her statement, I can ask my mother, "What did I do to make you think that I am lazy?" It may be that I forgot to do some chore early that morning. When I realize why she spoke of me in that manner, I can apologize for forgetting my chore. If there is no truth in what my mother has said, then I can quietly ignore the comment.

I learn to respond rather than react. I am aware. The sting is gone.

Moving from Blame to Compassion

When we feel violated by another's comment, we often respond by attacking or blaming the other. Unconsciously, we blame the other person, make him the villain and the source of our woes. We wish that the other person would change his ways, so we could feel better. Here is Tony De Mello's story.

Imagine a patient who goes to a doctor and relates his medical problem. The doctor responds, "Very well, I understand your symptoms. Do you know what I will do? I will prescribe a medicine for your neighbor!" The patient replies, "Thank you very much, doctor; that makes me feel much better."

Put this way, our wish for the other to change so we can feel better seems ridiculous. In fact, we are the ones who need the medicine, not the other whom we have unconsciously turned into the villain. Here is the medicine we need to take:

- Become aware of the behavior without evaluating or judging it.

- Separate the person and the behavior implied in the label.

- Become aware of the criteria implied in the judgment.

We need to practice these skills until they become comfortable.

The other person need not change or do anything different for us to see the behavior for what it is. He can continue in his ways, being who he is and doing what he does. It is only necessary for us to change. We need to learn to suspend evaluation and judgment.

Looking at this from a psychospiritual perspective, the other's comment threatens the core beliefs of the false self—for example, "I am worthwhile if am not lazy." The threat to the false self instantly triggers the physical fight or flight response. If we fight, we attack the other; if we take flight, we try to make the threat go away by distancing ourselves, blaming the other and wishing that the other person would learn to behave better, for example. At this point our false self is in control of the situation and the negative feelings we experience flag its presence. In awareness then, we can recognize the false self's panic and use our skills of observation without evaluation or judgment to lull the false self to sleep. When we do this, we can see the other more objectively, we see ourselves more objectively and we see the comment more objectively.

From this base of awareness, we may find it easy to act from compassion rather than blame. Bear in mind though, that no matter how practiced we are in awareness, we are likely to experience instantaneous hurt, anger and blame. Our first thought may be that *we* would feel better if only the *other person* would change. It is what we do next that determines whether we act from inner peace, strength and freedom or from turmoil, weakness and bondage.

By choosing to respond in awareness, we show respect for the other by suspending evaluation and judgment of his behavior and thereby respecting his person. By separating his behavior from his person, he may become less defensive and more receptive. It also helps us to understand the reasoning behind his behavior.

Just as you and I have intrinsic worth, so, too, do others. When we label them as good or bad, we violate their person. When we confuse their behavior with their person, we violate them. Whenever we regard others as a source of all our troubles, we violate them.

When we separate hateful behavior from the person, we may find ourselves experiencing compassion. We have the example of those who work with the most hardened criminals in prison and discover a genuine love for people who have committed abominable crimes. The movie *Dead Man Walking* is worth watching to see how even the most despised killer can be seen compassionately without excusing or mitigating his crime.

Once we realize that most behaviors are neutral and that they are culture-, context-, and situation-specific, then we will be more careful about judging ourselves and others. We become more open and more appreciative of the diversity in our lives. Diversity becomes an opportunity rather than a threat, and it brings about richness in our lives.

Key Points

- Our false self seeks security outside by adopting roles, positive labels and behaviors that are valued by our society.

• The security provided by the false self is fragile. If we lose our roles or positive labels, we loose our security.

• Our real security, as persons, is within. We all have inherent worth and dignity. It can't be taken away.

• Others can only threaten our security if we accept their negative judgments as a description of ourselves. By using the tools of awareness to separate our person from their judgment of our behavior, we become aware of our intrinsic worth, our true self.

• When we use awareness to separate person from behavior, compassion for that person may appear spontaneously. Our appreciation for the diverse people and cultures in our lives may increase.

A Word about the Exercises

Next, we give you two exercises that will help you discover how labels and roles unconsciously affect your life. You will first work on your own labels, then on the labels you give others.

You may want to refer to the section on Video Camera Language in Chapter 9 to help distinguish the label from the behavior. Labels generally involve a judgment and cannot be directly seen on a video tape. Behavior can.

Be gentle with yourself as you do this exercise. Approach it with a "no violence" attitude. Don't try to force anything to happen. Don't try to force yourself to feel or act in any particular way. Let what happens, happen.

EXERCISE
Exploring My Labels

1   Begin with a short awareness exercise. For example, focus on your breath for a few minutes.

2   Do the Coming Home exercise A for a few minutes. For example, repeat "Just perfect, just as I am."

3   Make a list of the labels you have been given as a child. The labels are usually worded as, "You are stubborn," or "You are energetic."

4   Choose one label to work on.

5   Become aware that the label indicates YOU = LABEL.

6   Become aware that the label is a short form or tag for certain behaviors.

7   Now convert the label into the behavior it represents. For example, "lazy" is converted into "My mother considers getting up at 9 instead of 6 as lazy." (You can check if it is a behavior by noting if a video camera would record it. If it does, then it is a behavior.)

8   Now restate your label in the following fashion: "You are lazy." becomes "I am worthwhile, just as I am. My mother considers my behavior of getting up at 9 instead of 6 as lazy."

9   Become aware of how you feel.

10   Repeat for other labels.

Take a "no violence" approach to the exercise. Do it gently.

Exploring How I Label Others

1   Begin with a short awareness exercise. For example, focus on your breath for a few minutes.

2   Do the Coming Home exercise A for a few minutes. For example, repeat "Just perfect, just as I am."

3   List the labels you give others.

4   Choose one label to work on.

5   Become aware that the label indicates YOU = LABEL.

6   Become aware that the label is a short form or tag for certain behaviors.

7   Now convert the label into the behavior it represents. For example, "lazy" is converted into, "I consider your behavior of getting up at 9 instead of 6 as lazy." (You can check if it is a behavior by checking if a video camera would record it. If it does, then it is a behavior.)

8   Now restate your label in the following fashion, "You are lazy," becomes "You are worthwhile, just as you are. I consider your behavior of getting up at 9 instead of 6 as lazy."

9   Become aware of how you feel.

10   Repeat for other labels you have given others.

Take a "no violence" approach to the exercise. Do it gently.

Chapter 11
RELATIONSHIPS

We humans are essentially social beings. We have an innate desire to relate to others. A child discovers who she is through her caregivers who become her mirrors. Through their behaviors towards her, verbal and nonverbal, she builds a sense of self. If the mirrors are distorting, then she is likely to develop a distorted image of self. In the future, the distorted image will affect all of her relationships.

In contrast, a genuine, growing relationship can lead to spiritual growth and a deeper awareness of ourselves and others. However, not all relationships lead to this deeper union because we interact with people for a number of reasons. We could relate to someone because we are needy and the other person meets those needs. We could also relate because we are attracted to the other's physical characteristics, behaviors, values, attitudes, etc.

The way we fall in love with someone is complex. When we say that we are attracted to someone, what we are saying is that our perception of the person matches some of the positive images our mind has accumulated over the years. The images could be related to any one or all of our sense modalities. This also explains why we are attracted to some and not to others. Beauty, indeed, is in the eyes of the beholder.

An Example

Let us look at the way we understand relationships. John loves Mary and Mary loves John. If we ask them about the feelings they experience when they are in this relationship, they might likely say they feel secure, wanted, valued, precious, good, loved, cared for, etc.

However, if for some unfortunate reason their relationship is broken, what are Mary and John likely to feel? They are likely to feel rejected, worthless, insecure, hurt, angry or depressed. Suicidal thoughts may pass through their minds.

If we were to ask them the cause of the negative feelings, they are likely to blame the other or themselves or circumstances. If we ask them who is responsible for the positive feelings they experienced in their relationship, they are likely to attribute them to the other. For example, Mary is likely to say, "John made me feel secure, wanted, precious, cared for, etc." John would say something similar.

The Magic Mirror

Let us explore this relationship through an image of a "magic mirror." Imagine that when we look in the mirror at our face, we feel we are handsome or pretty. However, when we withdraw from the mirror we feel the opposite—ugly or unattractive. Since this is a negative feeling, we want to avoid it. Every time we go before the mirror, we experience the positive feeling. However, every time we withdraw from the mirror we feel the opposite. We may conclude that the mirror makes us handsome or pretty. Since we attribute our good feelings to the mirror, we are likely to be dependent on the mirror to feel attractive. We would like to carry the mirror with us so that we can feel good all the time. We become attached to the mirror.

The above example looks silly because we know a mirror cannot make us handsome or pretty. It helps us discover our handsomeness or prettiness. When we realize this truth, we will not be attached to the mirror but remain grateful to the mirror for helping us to discover who we are. We may like to be with the mirror now and then, but we do not need the mirror to feel handsome or pretty. We feel better about ourselves, thanks to the mirror.

Codependent Relationships Imply Fear

Let us go back to our example of Mary and John. Mary and John are dependent on each other to feel good about themselves. The more they cling to each other, the more secure they feel with each other, and the more they feel loved. However, if Mary seems a little cold to John, then John is likely to feel insecure and fear will surface. This may make John cling to Mary more tightly.

When we analyze this relationship, we realize that this is a codependency relationship. Mary and John are both dependent on each other to feel good. They are likely to cling to each other. When there is some distance between the two, fear is likely to surface and lead to an immediate reaction of clinging tighter. This is the kind of relationship that is presented as love in numerous movies, novels and magazines. Dependency masquerades as love. It is not love at all.

Hidden deep underneath the dependency that masquerades as love is fear—the fear of being nobody, of being worthless. Often, we enter into relationships to cover this fear. We feel worthwhile because someone loves us. Unfortunately, the moment the other person withdraws, we return to feeling that we are nobody. A dependency relationship is like a cover used to hide our sense of worthlessness. It builds our false self with this belief: I am worthwhile because so and so loves me.

A Genuine Relationship
Can Lead to a Mystical Experience

In contrast, a genuine growing relationship is a mirroring relationship that helps us to discover our true Self. Let us explore this concept through the example of Mary and John. Why do they love each other? It is likely that they saw something beautiful in each other. Their verbal and nonverbal communication is a mirroring of what they see in each other. This process of mirroring can lead either to dependency or to freedom. If Mary says that she feels good because John loves her, then she is likely to become dependent on John. It is like saying that the mirror makes me handsome or pretty. However, if Mary were to begin to feel good about herself, thanks to the mirroring of John, then she is likely to feel more and more secure in herself. Similarly, John will begin to feel secure in himself, thanks to Mary's mirroring. Thus, instead of increasing dependence on each other, they become more and more secure in themselves and more free from each other. Now their love expression becomes more of a free gift, springing from love rather than fear.

Thanks to the mirroring of each other they discover their true Selves. In doing so, they may glimpse the grounding of the Self in the larger SELF, the divine or God. Thus, a genuine, growing, mirroring relationship can lead to a mystical experience, an awareness of our union with the divine. It makes us secure in who we are. We experience our connectedness with each other and with life itself at the deepest level—the union of Self in the larger SELF.

The opportunity for dependency or for mirroring exists in all our relationships: friend-friend, parent-child, boss-employee, teacher-student, etc. Since most relationships are based on the false self, whose basis is fear, they are by nature codependent. Using the skills of awareness and the exercises in this book, we may find our relationships shifting from dependency to mirroring. This shift may happen gradually, easily and without much effort as we grow in awareness and inner peace, strength and freedom.

Key Points

- We demonstrate our spirituality in the quality of our relationships with others. Conversely, our relationships can lead to spiritual growth or to a spiritual desert.

- A relationship based on mutual insecurity is rooted in the needs of our false self. If the needs are met, everything is fine. If the needs are not met, the relationship falls apart.

- A relationship based on mirroring, the mutual discovery of each partner's intrinsic worth and dignity, is rooted in the peace, strength and freedom of the true Self.

- Awareness can help us transform our relationships from dependency to mirroring. We must become aware of our own intrinsic "lovableness" before we can freely love another. Discovering our true Self helps us to love others more freely.

A Word about the Exercise

If your relationship is a dependency relationship, then we propose this exercise, which may not only free you from your dependency but also help you to find security in your true Self. That is, to come home.

Be gentle with yourself as you do this exercise. Approach it with a "no violence" attitude. Don't try to force anything to happen. Don't try to force yourself to feel or act in any particular way. Let what happens, happen.

Coming Home to Love

1   Make a list of people who loved you or love you.

2   Choose one from the list.

3   Imagine this person expressing his or her love to you, verbally or nonverbally. You are reliving your love experiences with this person.

4   You take in this person's love PASSIVELY. (In other words, you do not respond to this person.) You receive this person's love like a sponge, soaking in without responding.

5   When you feel saturated with this person's love, you tell yourself, I am lovable, I am precious, I am worthwhile, etc.

Take a "no violence" approach to the exercise. Do it gently.

Note: You can do this exercise whenever you feel low, lonely, etc. You can choose one person for several sittings. The effect of this exercise is the same as the Coming Home exercises.

FREQUENTLY ASKED QUESTIONS

1 *When I do the awareness exercises, my thoughts go all over the place, and I can't focus. I'm frustrated. What should I do? Maybe I'm not a meditator?*

Most of us have the difficulty you describe. This is because the false self is very active. When you do the awareness exercises and are present, observing without evaluation or judgment, then the false self will react with wild thoughts because you have stopped its regular operation. In the beginning, in a 30 minutes exercise you might find yourself in the exercise only for about 5-10 minutes. That is okay. As you continue doing it, you will spend more time in awareness.

However, if the thoughts continue to overwhelm you, then make the thoughts themselves the subject of your awareness exercise. For example, when you find yourself thinking, gently notice the thought, and say to yourself, "thinking." Then return to the focus of your exercise.

2 *The idea that I'm "just perfect, just as I am" is ridiculous to me. How can I be perfect when I have so many faults and difficulties in my life?*

Here you need to distinguish between your person and your behavior. Your person, as created by God, is perfect. You cannot alter or change your person. You can only grow in awareness of it. However, your behavior can be changed.

3 *I can't seem to get started on the quest exercise, "What do I want?" What should I do?"*

First, do not make it an intellectual exercise. This is the tendency of most people. Instead, let your response gently arise from within. If you get stuck, leave the exercise for the time being and revisit it later. Sometimes, it takes several sittings to go deeper into what one wants.

4 *I can understand that I may miss the truth of a situation because I don't see accurately what is going on, especially if the situation is emotional or threatening. Even if I practice awareness, how can I test if what I perceive is what is actually happening? How can I tell when I am fooling myself?*

There is no absolute guarantee that you are in touch with the truth of the situation. However, the freer we are inwardly, the more objectively we are able to see the situation. You may find the Using Awareness to Deal with Past Negative Experiences exercise (Chapter 8) particularly helpful. As we come home to our true self, we are able to view things with love. So, the best way of living in truth is to live at the self level.

5 *You say to stay in the present. I can't help reliving and revisiting some very painful events in my life. What should I do?*

Sometimes our past negative experiences can prevent us from being in the present. If your negative experience is not a trauma or phobia, then I suggest you do the exercise, Using Awareness to Deal with Past Negative Experiences (Chapter 8). If you suffer from serious trauma or phobia, you may need professional help to overcome the experience.

6   *Does staying in the present mean ignoring the future?*
    Are you advocating being a Pollyanna?
Not at all. We need to plan for the future. However, the act of planning takes place in the present. Sometimes, we use our hopes and fears for the future to escape from the unpleasant present. This is not helpful.

7   *Should I not think of the past or the future?*
It is often necessary to consider the past and the future, but do that in the present and be aware of it.

8   *When I try to observe an event objectively I find myself getting upset and angry. What should I do?*
When this happens, you need to analyze your experience slowly.

a   You are upset.

b   You are experiencing negative feelings.

c   Your false self is threatened, which means a belief is threatened.

d   Identify the belief by asking, What do I want instead? Whatever comes up is the object of your belief.

e   Come to Self level by doing either of the Coming Home exercises (Chapters 6 or 7) and then look at the event again.

9   *Does observing without evaluation or judgment mean that I must drop my standards of right and wrong? Isn't it spineless?*
Our evaluation and judgment are based on criteria developed over the years through social conditioning. Most of the time, we are unaware of the judgment, evaluations or criteria, and this leads to automatic, unconscious reactions to people and events. When we

observe without evaluation or judgment, we go beyond the criteria and see things as they are. However, we do need criteria to operate in society. But we need to hold them lightly not tightly. When we do that, we have our principles but we can easily see things from other people's perspective.

10 *Should I not evaluate sometimes? How can we live without it?*

Yes we do evaluate and we need to sometimes. The awareness exercises help us to go beyond evaluations and see things as they are. For example, imagine you have to evaluate the performance of an employee. The employee is a wonderful person but his work does not meet the criteria and expectations of the firm. Maybe he will do well in another firm. In this example, there is a distancing between your task of evaluation and yourself. Secondly, there is a separation between the person and his performance and thirdly, it is situation specific. When we evaluate here, we are essentially saying that his behavior does not match the criteria and expectations of the firm. That is the reality. How he will perceive it is another matter and may require compassion on your part.

11 *I'm not aware that fear plays any role in my life as a mature adult, yet you make a big deal of it. Am I an exception?*

Most of us have succeeded in finding ways to mask and cope with our unconscious fears. As long as you feel secure, you will not experience fear. However, when your false self is threatened, fear will surface in the form of negative feelings. Negative feelings, like instant anger or sadness, are a clue to our hidden fears. As we become aware of our negative feelings, fears and beliefs, they tend to evaporate. Our life becomes more peaceful.

12 *Is fear bad?*

Not at all. Fear is useful for survival. If we had no fear, we might step into traffic without looking. Unfortunately, our brain is not able to distinguish between threats to our physical survival and threats to our beliefs. It reacts with fear as if our physical survival is threatened when only our false self is threatened.

13 *Is fear responsible for the violence in the world?*

Yes, all violence comes from fear. Often it is a result of threat to one's false self rather than physical survival. The threat may be to the false self of an individual, an organization or a nation.

14 *You ask us to go back to childhood to examine our beliefs. Haven't we put these childish things in our past? I'm a grown up and what my parents said or didn't say doesn't affect me today.*

The beliefs we have developed in our childhood are internalized. What you may have dropped may be your childish behaviors. The beliefs form the structure of our false self's security system. They operate automatically and unconsciously. Some people cannot recall traumas they experienced in their childhood, yet these events continue to unconsciously influence their behavior and feelings.

15 *Isn't the ego or false self so much psychobabble? Isn't this about right and wrong and universal truths?*

First of all, the ego we are talking about is not the ego of Freud and other psychologists. It is a concept found in mystical writings of many traditions and corresponds closely to the findings of modern psychology. It refers to a false image we develop about ourselves throughout our life, beginning in early childhood. We now realize that our notions of right, wrong and universal truth are rooted in these beliefs.

16 *Can we get rid of the ego or false self?*

No. As long as we have the mind, we cannot get rid of the false self. However, when we are at the Self level, we can laugh at the false self and not take it seriously. It loses its power. The best example of this is about the person who is dreaming of the tiger and is terrified and because of his fear, he wakes up. When he wakes up, he realizes that there is no tiger and he laughs.

17 *Can I at least become secure in my true Self?*

Yes and no. As you continue to practice, you will begin to feel more and more secure. This does not mean that you will not go to the false self level often. Remember, false self is our default. When we become aware that we have slipped into the false self, we can use the skills we have practiced to move more quickly to the Self level.

18 *I feel down and blue a lot of the time. Is this my nature?*
      Am I just moody?

Your moodiness may come from a number of sources. That does not mean that you are your moods. First, it means that for some reason your false self does not feel secure. Second, you are not experiencing the joy of being at the Self level. You have feelings; you are not your feelings.

19 *Must I do all of these exercises? Do I need to repeat the*
      exercises? If so, which ones? How often?

Since our default is the false self, we need to practice awareness until it becomes a strong skill. You don't necessarily have to do all of the exercises. Concentrate on the basic awareness exercise, Coming Home (Chapters 6 and 7) and Using Awareness to Deal with Past Negative Experiences (Chapter 8). It's helpful to repeat these core exercises often. Daily for 20 minutes is the usual recommendation. As you practice you will become more skillful. Then it will be easy to use them whenever a negative situation arises.

20 *Try as I may I don't get anything out of the Coming Home exercises (Chapter 6 or 7), which you say is a foundation. Any suggestions?*

First of all, you need to check if you are doing the exercise as the instructions recommend. The main focus is repeating the phrase consciously and letting yourself experience what you are saying. If you are just beginning and are experiencing resistance, that is normal. It is like having lived all your life in a slum and now you discover that you have a beautiful home. At first, you will not feel at home in your home. You need to give yourself some time.

21 *Do I have to believe in a personal God to get anything out of this book?*

No, you do not have to believe in the concept of God to enjoy this book. Different people have different concepts or names for a reality that is beyond our self. Alcoholics Anonymous has a saying, "The only thing you need to know about the higher power is that it isn't you."

22 *Self/SELF doesn't make sense to me. Should I stop now?*

Please continue practicing the Coming Home exercises (Chapter 6 and 7); they provide a first-hand experience for the concepts we labor to describe. Perhaps, reading the earlier chapters again might help you to understand the concept of the true self grounded in the larger SELF.

23 *I don't get the psychospiritual framework. Are we all basically good inside? Or bad inside and in need of salvation?*

Yes, we are all basically good. However, we are not aware of it. Salvation is discovering the simple truth of who we are. The great religious leaders make us aware of this truth.

24 *You say we must separate person and behavior. Isn't it appropriate to judge a person by what he or she does? Isn't Hitler, for example, intrinsically bad?*

We do need to separate person from behavior. As we mentioned earlier, a person is sacred but his or her behaviors may be right or wrong, depending on the context. Our behaviors may flow from our false self or Self. In other words, they may flow from fear or love. When we are operating at the false self level, we are in the survival mode. A panic button is pressed because we were not aware of the true Self. The great villains of history had intrinsic worth as persons, as we all do. Generally they were driven by their fear and false self to behave in destructive ways.

25 *I'm proud of my role as a teacher. It adds meaning to my life. Are you saying it isn't important?*

Oh no! Your role as a teacher is very important but it is still just a role. You are not the role. It is not your identity. Your identity is your true Self. Roles consist of behaviors that will flow from love if you are operating at the Self level.

26 *What is the role of religious belief in your framework?*

This book is not about religion at all. It is a guide to spiritual peace and strength that can be used by people of any religion or none.

27 *Is awareness prayer?*

Yes. Any means, technique or method that leads us to an awareness of our true Self is prayer.

28 *What do we do with the traditional prayers we have learned?*

Prayers can be a means to come to the Self level and experience
its security. Notice if your prayers lead you to your true Self. If they
do not, then you may need to modify them. You may need some
guidance here. If after doing all this you still feel your prayers are not
helpful, then you need to seek more meaningful and helpful prayers.

29 *What is the role of a community?*

We are social beings and we need the help and support of others
in this journey to Self. There are times when we want to celebrate this
experience. Our common prayers can be an expression of this joy. As
corporal beings, we feel the need to express together what is going on
within. Being at the Self level fosters a sense of community, not isola-
tion. We feel more and more connected with others at a deeper level.

30 *If we are all mystics, then why do we indulge in violence?*

We are all mystics, and we are all in a relationship with the divine.
But unfortunately, we are not aware of who we are. All violence
comes from fear. All violence originates from ignorance of our true
Self. Therefore, growth in awareness of who we are leads to nonviolence.

31 *Is suffering an unavoidable part of our lives?*

We need to distinguish between pain and suffering. Often, the
terms are used interchangeably. Suffering is mental while pain is
physical. Suffering is linked to the false self and pain is linked to the
physical body. Suffering occurs when our false self is threatened.
When we live at the Self level, we do not need to suffer. Some pain
is inevitable in life; the suffering is *not*.

ADDITIONAL RESOURCES

Aronson, Elliot. 1988. *Social Animal.* New York: W.H. Freeman and Company, pg. 113-114.
A reference to the social experiment described in Chapter 2.

Barks, Coleman. 1997. *Essential Rumi.* San Francisco: Harper.
A vivid translation of classic poems of Sufi mysticism dating from thirteenth century Persia.

Chodron, Pema. 2004. *Getting Unstuck: Breaking Your Habitual Patterns & Encountering Naked Reality.* (Audio CD). Louisville, CO: Sounds True.
Recorded talks on meditation and awareness from one of the first Americans ordained as a Buddhist nun.

Chodron, Pema. 2002. *When Things Fall Apart: Heart Advice for Difficult Times.* Boston: Shambhala.
Thoughtful and classic meditation exercises for times of stress.

The Dalai Lama and Howard C. Cutler. 1998. *The Art of Happiness: A Handbook for Living.* New York: Riverhead.
Cutler is a psychiatrist who casts Buddhist thought into a western perspective.

The Dalai Lama. 2001. *An Open Heart: Practicing Compassion in Everyday Life.* Boston: Little, Brown.
A practical guide to useful Buddhist practices.

De Mello, Anthony. 1990. *Awareness*. New York: Image.
Read this book. It's De Mello at his sauciest on the need for awareness.

De Mello, Anthony. 1984. *Sadhana*. New York: Image.
A systematic series of spiritual exercises.

De Mello, Anthony. 1984. *Song of the Bird*. New York: Image.
These lively short stories will have you puzzling about the heart of spirituality.

De Mello, Anthony. 1992. *The Way to Love*. New York: Doubleday.
Penetrating essays on the nature of love.

Finley, James. 1978. *Merton's Palace of Nowhere*. Notre Dame, IN: Ave Maria Press.
De Mello was influenced by this summary of Merton's thought.

Goldberg, Natalie. 1996. *Writing Down the Bones*. Boston: Shambhala.
An introduction to writing as a means of Zen awareness and meditation.

Hanh, Thich Nhat. 1997. *Living Buddha, Living Christ*. New York: Riverhead.
A Zen master's reflections on Buddhism and Christianity.

Hanh, Thich Nhat. 1996. *The Miracle of Mindfulness*. Boston: Beacon Press.
A clear introduction to awareness and mindfulness.

Hanh, Thich Nhat. 1992. *Peace Is Every Step: The Path of Mindfulness in Everyday Life*. New York: Bantam.
An introduction to walking meditation, an ancient Zen practice.

Hesse, Hermann. 1951. *Siddhartha*. New York: New Directions.
See this book for the complete story told in Chapter 1.

Kabat-Zinn, Jon. 1994. *Wherever You Go, There You Are: Mindfulness Meditation in Everyday Life*. New York: Hyperion.
A witty guide from a medical stress-reduction perspective.

Keating, Thomas. 1994. *Open Mind, Open Heart: The Contemplative Dimension of the Gospel*. New York: Continuum.
The definitive introduction to centering prayer as meditation.

Levine, Stephen and Ondrea Levine. 1994. *Embracing the Beloved: Relationship as a Path of Awakening*. New York: Doubleday.
If you liked Chapter 11, read this book.

May, Gerald. 1993. *Simply Sane: The Spirituality of Mental Health*. New York: Crossroad/Herder & Herder.
This classic influenced De Mello's view of spirituality.

Merton, Thomas. 1961. *New Seeds of Contemplation*. New York: New Directions.
Merton's advice to young monks is his finest expression of personal spirituality.

Oliver, Mary. 1986. *Dream Work*. New York: The Atlantic Monthly Press.
The poem, "Wild Geese," reflects many of the themes of this book.

St. Ignatius. 2000. *The Spiritual Exercises of St. Ignatius*. New York: Vintage.
This classic dating from 1541 is best encountered through a guided retreat.

Appendix 1:
GUIDED MEDITATIONS

As you work through each chapter, you may want to try one of the following recorded meditations, which are available for purchase at our website www.BroadbandLiving.org. Each meditation begins with a brief awareness exercise and continues with a guided fantasy meditation. They are intended as a supplement to, not a replacement for, the exercises in each chapter.

Chapter	GUIDED MEDITATION
1	QUEST: Self-Surrender
2	TRUTH: Peeling the Onion
3	AWARENESS: The Mountain Lake, Communing with Nature
4	FEAR: Liberation
5	THE FALSE SELF: The River
6	THE TRUE SELF: Footprints
7	THE LARGER SELF: Ocean
8	A PSYCHOSPIRITUAL FRAMEWORK: Worship
9	PERSON AND BEHAVIOR: The Gift
10	LABELS, ROLES AND IDENTITY: The Seed
11	RELATIONSHIPS: Temple

Appendix 2:
SUMMARY OF KEY POINTS

PART ONE
Becoming Aware

Chapter 1: **Quest**

- Inner growth begins with a profound question, "What do I really want?"

- We tend to look outside ourselves for what we think we want—money, fame, love.

- We tend to get stuck looking for what we want.

- What we want, true happiness, is inside.

Chapter 2: **Truth**

- The path of truth is to directly experience ourselves, the world and others as they actually are, not as we believe them to be.

- This path of truth involves being aware of ourselves—our feelings, our thoughts and our behaviors—without evaluation or judgment.

- To do so, we must be willing to let go of many of the things and beliefs that make us feel secure. The price of truth is security.

- Through a process of conditioning we have developed a security system that operates automatically and mostly unconsciously.

- When truth threatens our security, we often cope by rationalizing or justifying ourselves.

- The truth will set us free.

Chapter 3: **Awareness**

- Awareness is the path to truth—to see things as they are.

- Awareness is

  - being in the present

  - observing without evaluation or judgment.

- Awareness is a skill that can be discovered and developed.

- Skill is developed by frequent practice of any of the awareness exercises.

Chapter 4: **Fear**

- Coming face to face with our deepest fears is a hallmark of spiritual maturity.

- Threats to our security trigger a fight or flight response that instantly affects brain and body function, temporarily overpowering the rational mind. The fight or flight response is essential for our physical survival.

- Purely psychological threats to our sense of security can produce profound fight or flight responses, even though they are not real. That is, they do not threaten our physical survival.

- Fear is a powerful motivator, a means of controlling others and the unconscious basis for much of our behavior.

- Our conditional messages in childhood make us feel we are not okay, which generates fear.

- Unconsciously, we work hard to cover up and avoid threats to our sense of security by following society's suggestions to make ourselves secure.

- Our negative feelings are flags warning us that our sense of security has been threatened.

PART TWO
Coming Home to Our True Self

Chapter 5: **The False Self**

- Our false self or ego is a mental construct devoted to preserving a sense of self-worth.

- The false self is imaginary, consisting of unconscious beliefs about what will preserve its sense of self-worth.

- When the false self's beliefs are threatened, it reacts as if its existence were threatened. It triggers a physical fight or flight response that is instant, automatic and often unconscious. We usually notice strong negative feelings when this happens.

- We often operate under the unconscious influence of the false self, gaining a positive identity through the roles, behavior and labels we assume.

- The security gained by the false self beliefs is fragile. If we lose our role, we can lose our identity.

Discovering AWARENESS

- We can't get rid of the false self. It's a construct of the mind, deeply ingrained and unconscious. As long as we have our minds, we'll have our false self.

- Negative feelings indicate that the false self is in control. We can use them as flags.

- Awareness practice can loosen the false self grip and provide us with real security.

Chapter 6: **The True Self**

- As we lull the false self to sleep by suspending judgment and evaluation, we begin to glimpse and wake up to the core of our being, the true Self.

- Each of us has intrinsic worth. This is the true Self.

- The self is who we are, just as we are, absent of any judgment or evaluation—a human, complete, whole, a masterpiece.

- We share this ground of being with all other living things.

Chapter 7: **The Larger Self**

- Experiencing the true Self, that is glimpsing ourselves as we really are, often leads to a sense of connection to everyone and everything.

- We refer to this common ground of all beings as the larger SELF.

- Mystics throughout the ages and throughout the world struggle to express this experience.

- In a spiritual and mystic sense, this is what we mean by the SELF.

Chapter 8: **A Psychospiritual Framework**

- We are worthwhile just as we are. This is our true Self.

- Unaware of this, our false self tries to make us worthwhile by means of a system of unconscious beliefs based on conditional messages. "You are worthwhile, if … ."

- Inner peace, strength and freedom, depends on us discovering our true Self and, as a result, slowly letting go of our false self. True spirituality is a process of discovering who we truly are.

- For us, spirituality is to see ourselves as we truly are and to see others as they truly are. In theistic terms, to see ourselves through God's eyes and as a result we begin to see others as God sees them. It is a process of discovering rather than becoming.

- The path of discovery is to slowly, piece by piece, loosen the hold of the false self through the tools of awareness.

- As awareness loosens the grip of the false self and its beliefs, our perspective changes. We begin to see ourselves and others without judging. Love and nonviolence begin to happen. We begin to have a deeper experience of harmony with nature and greater inner freedom.

PART THREE

Applications to Everyday Life

Chapter 9: **Person and Behavior**

- Our person has intrinsic dignity and worth. It is our true Self. The worth does not depend on how we behave or how we or others judge us.

- Our behavior can be observed without judgment or evaluation. This is what a video camera does. Capturing what is. Nothing more, nothing less.

- Judgments of our behavior are based on the criteria that are usually determined by our society. They can be useful or the source of prejudice, discrimination and violence.

- A critical skill in awareness is to clearly distinguish between the person (who always has dignity) and the behavior (which may be judged as good or bad.)

- Exercises can help us build our awareness skills so that the distinction between person and behavior is natural, quick and effective.

Chapter 10: **Labels, Roles and Identity**

- Our false self seeks security outside by adopting roles, positive labels and behaviors that are valued by our society.

- The security provided by the false self is fragile. If we lose our roles or positive labels, we lose our security.

- Our real security, as persons, is within. We all have inherent worth and dignity. It can't be taken away.

- Others can only threaten our security if we accept their negative judgments as a description of ourselves. By using the tools of awareness to separate our person from their judgment of our behavior, we become aware of our intrinsic worth, our true Self.

- When we use awareness to separate person from behavior, compassion for that person may appear spontaneously. Our appreciation for the diverse people and cultures in our lives may increase.

Chapter 11: **Relationships**

- We demonstrate our spirituality in the quality of our relationships with others. Conversely, our relationships can lead to spiritual growth or to a spiritual desert.

- A relationship based on mutual insecurity is rooted in the needs of our false self. If the needs are met, everything is fine. If the needs are not met, the relationship falls apart.

- A relationship based on mirroring, the mutual discovery of each partner's intrinsic worth and dignity, is rooted in the peace, strength and freedom of the true Self.

- Awareness can help us transform our relationships from dependency to mirroring. We must become aware of our own intrinsic "lovableness" before we can freely love another. Discovering our true Self helps us to love others more freely.

Discovering AWARENESS

INDEX